More advance praise for
The Corporate Blogging Book

"The first clear-eyed look at the what and how of blogging as a corporate communications strategy. Both entertaining and informative, Debbie Weil's book allays fears surrounding blogging and provides sensible advice on how to write an effective blog, who should write it, and how to measure success. This excellent primer will satisfy even the most skeptical of managers. If you fear you'll get it wrong, this book is the best place to start in order to get it right!"
—Rich Marcello, senior vice president and general manager,
Business Critical Servers, Hewlett Packard

"As an author and speaker on customer service, I am constantly talking to corporate America about being more responsive to the people who buy their products and services. Establish a dialogue with customers. That's where corporate blogging comes in. Using humor, insight, opinion, and fact, Debbie Weil has produced an invaluable handbook for starting—and sustaining—the conversation between buyers and sellers."

—Robert Spector, author of
The Nordstrom Way to Customer Service Excellence

"Debbie is at the forefront of one of the most important forces affecting corporate America: how to harness the online conversation to help build authentic and deeper connections with your customers. Most companies don't yet get it; those who read this book will. Those who don't are doomed over the long term."
—Paul Rosenfeld, general manager, QuickBooks Online Edition

"Debbie's book is a great introduction to corporate blogging. If you are thinking about a corporate blog and want to learn the terrain, here is help to get started. Also useful if you are a manager who is scared or concerned about employees' blogging. I had already been doing an 'executive blog' for six months when I read Debbie's book, but I still found it informative and interesting."

—Dave Hitz, founder and executive vice president, NetApp

"There's far too much hype about blogs and not enough real-world explanation about the why and how. Debbie Weil's book is finally a step in the right direction. This is an easy-to-read, easy-to-understand, easy-to-implement, plain-truth type of book that will be invaluable to any company starting a blog."

—Kevin W. Holland, division vice president,
Business Operations & Membership,
Air Conditioning Contractors of America

"An excellent primer for the uninitiated, this book explains convincingly and clearly how to embrace customers in this casual online conversation."

—Jeremiah Owyang, global Web marketing strategist

"Debbie Weil demystifies blogging in simple, practical language. Rather than push you into it, she gently explains, coaxes, and leads you by the hand so you can jump right in."

—Irving Wladawsky-Berger, vice president
Technical Strategy and Innovation, IBM

The
Corporate
Blogging
Book

The Corporate Blogging Book

Absolutely Everything You Need to Know to Get It Right

Debbie Weil

With a foreword by Bob Lutz,
global vice chairman of
General Motors (and blogger)

PORTFOLIO

PORTFOLIO
Published by the Penguin Group
Penguin Group (USA) Inc., 375 Hudson Street, New York, New York 10014, U.S.A.
Penguin Group (Canada), 90 Eglinton Avenue East, Suite 700, Toronto, Ontario,
Canada M4P 2Y3 (a division of Pearson Penguin Canada Inc.)
Penguin Books Ltd, 80 Strand, London WC2R ORL, England
Penguin Ireland, 25 St. Stephen's Green, Dublin 2, Ireland (a division of Penguin Books Ltd)
Penguin Books Australia Ltd, 250 Camberwell Road, Camberwell, Victoria 3124, Australia
(a division of Pearson Australia Group Pty Ltd)
Penguin Books India Pvt Ltd, 11 Community Centre, Panchsheel Park,
New Delhi – 110 017, India
Penguin Group (NZ), Cnr Airborne and Rosedale Roads, Albany, Auckland 1310,
New Zealand (a division of Pearson New Zealand Ltd)
Penguin Books (South Africa) (Pty) Ltd, 24 Sturdee Avenue, Rosebank,
Johannesburg 2196, South Africa

Penguin Books Ltd, Registered Offices: 80 Strand, London WC2R ORL, England

First published in 2006 by Portfolio, a member of Penguin Group (USA) Inc.

1   3   5   7   9   10   8   6   4   2

Publisher's Note

This publication is designed to provide accurate and authoritative information in regard to the subject matter covered. It is sold with the understanding that the publisher is not engaged in rendering legal, accounting or other professional services. If you require legal advice or other expert assistance, you should seek the services of a competent professional.

LIBRARY OF CONGRESS CATALOGING-IN-PUBLICATION DATA
Weil, Debbie.
    The corporate blogging book : absolutely everything you need to know to get it right /
Debbie Weil ; with a foreword by Bob Lutz.
      p.   cm.
    ISBN 1-59184-125-9
    1. Business communication—Blogs.   2. Blogs.   I. Title.
HD30.37.W45 2006
659.20285'4678—dc22   2006043469

Printed in the United States of America
Set in Garamond 3
Designed by Joseph Rutt, Level C

For Sam
and
Eliza, Timothy and Amanda

Contents

Foreword

I entered the auto business in 1962 fresh out of business school. After over 40 years in the business, I can safely say that it has been a wonderful ride. While many of the most important elements of this industry remain constant—things such as design, styling, ride, comfort, handling and safety—our ability to reach new levels of achievement in each of these disciplines never ceases to amaze me. Please consider the vast improvements in recent years in safety, reliability, fuel economy and emissions as basic examples.

In direct contrast to this constant innovation in the design, engineering and manufacturing processes, the methods with which we communicate to our core constituencies have remained fundamentally the same. Sure, corporate communications has become slicker and more manipulative and advertising has often become increasingly obnoxious in an attempt to break through the clutter, but that's about it.

Of course, many of you will say, "What about the Internet, it has changed everything." Well, I'm certainly not an Internet expert, but I would argue that, despite the influence of the Internet on purchasing decisions, most major companies still communicate using the same sterile, safe techniques they've used in the more traditional venues since I began my career.

So on one hand, you have companies that have hardly changed the way they communicate in the last 40 years. On the other hand, you have a media ecosystem that is increasingly dependent on sensationalism, brutal competition, and the rehashing of conventional wisdom. Enter blogging.

I've always been a prolific writer. Until now, the victims of my frequent prose outbursts have been my colleagues and friends. On occasion, a memo or two leaked to the media and made for a juicy story. But I can't tell you how many times I felt handcuffed when a story broke that was blatantly untrue. (At least in my opinion!)

Not anymore. When the idea of blogging was first presented to me, I jumped at the opportunity to opine and to converse. For me, that's what it's all about: telling a story as I see it, without a filter, and in turn, receiving unvarnished feedback.

We had no idea what to expect when we launched the GM Fast-Lane Blog. Remarkably, we had 5,000 visitors on our first day. Since then, we've received thousands of comments and have engaged in countless conversations both online and offline. We've connected with thousands of people we otherwise would not have reached.

To be successful, it is extremely important that a business blogger have a solid understanding of what is acceptable and what isn't. The blogosphere is littered with corpses!

For some time, it has been my belief that blogging isn't for everyone. If you're linguistically challenged or extremely sensitive, don't blog!

For those of you who are neither of the above, this book provides a more substantive body of opinion, analysis and advice to aid your decision-making process. Debbie Weil gets into the trenches with some of the best corporate blogs. I advise you to climb in there with her to get the compelling backstory (just as you would on a blog) of how it's really done. Of course, you may be asking whether blogging is useful or relevant when your organization is in a period of crisis. My answer to that is yes. It's more important than ever to open the door wide, speak as honestly as possible and listen to your customers.

One final word of advice: If you feel blogging is right for you or your company, don't spend your precious hours seeking the approvals of an endless body of corporate stakeholders. Launch your blog and watch the conversation unfold.

> Bob Lutz
> Vice Chairman,
> Global Product Development
> General Motors

Introduction

"Real people don't blog."
—Anonymous

This is a book about blogging. And because transparency and authenticity are two of the touchstones that make the blogosphere go round, I'd better come clean. The statement above really isn't anonymous. My husband made it.

Now, Sam is a wonderful guy and if you're a marketer he's probably just the kind of person you want to reach: he's a highly educated professional, he has disposable income, and he goes online more and more these days to buy stuff (at least, I think that's where all the new golf gear is coming from). But he doesn't blog. He doesn't even read blogs.

As he said to me ever so politely as I was finishing this book, "Anyone who blogs is a chronic complainer or a contrarian or someone who just wants to hear the sound of his own voice, right?" Wow. I sat back on my heels to wrap my head around his words. So that's what he was thinking during the months I was writing?

First, the stats. In mid-2005, 40 to 60 percent of U.S. Internet users didn't know what a blog was, according to eMarketer.com. Though the not-in-the-know population has been shrinking fast, of those who *had* heard the term, many thought of blogs as online diaries for anxiety-ridden teenagers.

So maybe Sam isn't a bad proxy for a lot of folks out there. Are you one of them? Are you wondering what this whole blogging thing is about, and specifically how it relates to your business or organization (large or small)? If so, this book is for you. If you're already on the blogging bandwagon and want to learn how to *deliver* on the promise of this remarkable new communications tool, this book is for you too.

We're entering an age of more open, honest and authentic corporate communications. Blogs are a key enabler of this new way of talking with customers, employees, the media and other constituencies. Packaged, filtered, controlled conversations are out. Open, two-way, less-than-perfect communications with your customers and employees are in. It's as if big business has finally caught up with the baby boomer's approach to relationships and to parenting. Listen, learn, debate, be willing to change, admit mistakes, be equals with your children, be fair to others with whom you have an adversarial relationship. Acting like a dictator will get you nowhere.

This book goes behind the scenes to reveal the story of how mega corporations such as Boeing, GM, HP, Intel and Sun Microsystems are creating original editorial products—i.e., *blogs!*—as a way to communicate more effectively and more deeply with customers and employees. Ideally, blogging enables these companies to influence opinion, to tap into the expertise, ideas and clear thinking of their core constituencies—and to treat employees and customers like friends rather than foes.

This book will uncover how these corporate blogs got started, what the nitty-gritty is of keeping them going, what the risks are, what the biggest challenges are, what the results are . . . and what we can look forward to. This is a book about the resurrection of the craft of writing, the power and excitement of raw, honest communication and the willingness and courage of a small number of large corporations to humbly listen and learn from their customers.

I'll promise to keep existential ramblings about blogging to a minimum: *Blogs will change everything. Blog or die!* . . . It's still early days. Too soon to predict how widespread the corporate blogging phenomenon will be. But one thing is clear: blogging is one symptom—or result—of the new bottom-up business ecosystem that is beginning to emerge.

I'm here as your guide, to answer the kind of sensible questions that results-oriented businesspeople tend to ask: We've got a Web site—why do we need a blog? What's the difference? How will a blog be useful to our business? How does a blog fit into our overall marketing strategy? How much time does it take to maintain a blog? Who in our company should write it? And of course, will blogging affect our bottom line? What business results can we expect?

This book will demystify blogging. I've organized it so you'll start with a bit of context, what blogging is, how it crossed over from personal to business use and why you need to become fluent with this new communications channel. Subsequent chapters address the concerns I've heard over and over from managers and executives: what about the time it takes? Legal risks? Guidelines? Should our CEO be blogging? What topics should we cover?

Along the way, I'll give you lots of examples of what companies large and small are doing with blogs. Feel free to steal from their ideas and experiences for your own blogging efforts. You'll also hear directly from a number of experienced corporate bloggers who have been writing or managing blogs. I'll introduce you to the most useful blogging tools and technologies—as well as podcasts and wikis—so you'll understand what they can do and how you might use them.

Finally, I've included a cheat sheet of sorts (in chapter 9) to help you make the case for blogging to your boss. Or other key stakeholders. We'll end with a brief look into the (near) future. I'll pose some key questions: are the Web and the Internet finally maturing to the point that they're an inextricable part of your customers' lives? Is blogging in and of itself revolutionary? Is it merely a symptom of a new way of doing business?

You can help me answer these questions. I want to hear from you! Visit the accompanying book blog at TheCorporateBloggingBook. com. Feel free to leave your comments and queries.

Ready, set, go.

CHAPTER 1

Top Twenty Questions About Corporate Blogging

So much chatter. So many blogs. So little time. The blogging phenomenon has reached critical mass. The tipping point for "wait and see" is swinging, like a metronome, toward "better do something now." But where do you start? What, really, does blogging mean as a marketing, PR and corporate communications strategy? If you fear that entering the blogosphere is like tiptoeing into a minefield—where you're bound to trip an explosion of controversy or criticism—how can you learn to do it *right*?

Let's begin with the facts, the FAQs. Here are the top twenty questions I hear most often when I am talking to managers and executives about corporate blogging. (I use the terms "company" and "customer" throughout the book. Substitute "organization" and "member" if that works better for you.) Consider these guideposts for the rest of the book. In fact, if you want a quick synopsis of the world of blogging as it relates to business, read just this chapter and you'll be able to go back to the office and sound reasonably knowledgeable. Really. I won't be offended.

1. WHAT IS CORPORATE BLOGGING?

Corporate blogging is the use of blogs to further organizational goals. It's the co-opting by the big dogs of a communications tool that has been successfully used by the little guys. Picture an e-newsletter, a viral marketing campaign, an open channel through which your customers can talk to you and your own news station all rolled up into one. Now wrap that into a low-cost, easy-to-use, always-fresh Web site. That's what effective corporate blogging is.

Blogs can be public and found by anyone searching the Web. Or they can be inward-facing, for company use only. Internal blogs are increasingly used for project management and information sharing. It doesn't matter what shape, stripe or size your organization is: for-profit or non-profit, Fortune 500, SME (small to medium-sized enterprise), small business or solopreneur. There are dozens of ways you can use a blog.

Oh, and a quick definition: on a practical level, a blog, short for "Web log," is an easy-to-publish Web site. A blog is written in an informal, conversational style that tells the "real" story. No puffery, no PR. Individual bloggers—who have largely defined the blogosphere—often use an edgy voice, dish out uncensored opinion and spread information that is not necessarily accurate. But don't dismiss them! Some of these bloggers may be your customers.

Now put on your marketing hat. Think bigger. A blog is a marketing communications channel. Picture what you might use it for. Your goals can be long-term and loose, such as improved internal communications or a closer connection with your customers. Or short-term and specific: an event, a campaign, a deadline-driven software project. Corporate blogs can be sanctioned, even encouraged, by the boss and written by individual employees. Or managed, formally, by the corporate communications department. They can be written by non-employees known as customer evangelists—customers who love your company, products and services so much they spread the word for you. Sometimes the CEO or other senior executives develop a flair for blogging.

Business blogging has become a broader, muddier term. It encompasses corporate blogging. It also includes the new generation of media companies that publish networks of blogs supported by advertising. And a small number of independent bloggers who earn a living directly from their blogs, as self-publishers, by running ads. In fact a whole new segment of online advertising has grown up around blogs. Business blogging is shorthand for "So what's the business model? How do we make money with this thing?"

Corporate blogging, in contrast, is not usually about making a quick buck. Corporate blogging is a communications and marketing channel, but with a twist—it's two-way. You can't foresee precisely what results you'll get by using it, although the positive usually outweighs the negative. And, again ideally, this channel connects you to a noisy, ragged, global conversation—the blogosphere.

2. THE BLOGO-WHAT??

The blogosphere. It's a big, loud place. It's the universe of blogs. It's "the virtual realm of blogdom as a whole," as the *New York Times* called it.[1] With an estimated 80,000 blogs being created worldwide every day, by the end of 2006 the total number will approach or surpass 80 million. That's based on blog search company Technorati's forecast in mid-2005 that the number of blogs was doubling every five and a half months.[2] As yet, corporate blogs make up a tiny fraction of this number. Less than 5 percent, according to a June 2005 report by eMarketer.com on business blogging.

Of course, counting blogs is rapidly becoming a quaint practice. Remember a decade ago when we used to monitor the number of Web sites? Beginning in June 1993, Netscape's "What's New" page reported, each day, every new site worth visiting. An entry on September 28, 1993 noted: "Stanford University now has a home page" with a link to the new stanford.edu site. Only two years later, in 1995, Larry Page and Sergey Brin met at Stanford and began the collaboration that resulted in Google, Inc. (How short the history of the Web is!) By 2000, almost every large company had a Web site. In early 2005, 7 percent of U.S. Internet users had created a blog, although 62 percent didn't know what blogs were.[3]

It's what goes on *inside* the blogosphere that distinguishes it from being merely a collection of interactive Web sites. Daily, hourly, by the minute, millions of conversations are taking place. On individual blogs (between the publisher and the readers) and between blogs (when bloggers reference other bloggers). Bloggers are posting new written entries as well as audio and video. Readers and other bloggers are commenting on what's being said or shown. The ripple— or snowball—effect is huge and immediate.

The blogosphere is often called a collective conversation. Think of it "as communities where information, links, opinions, videos, audio files, photos and other forms of media are easily and frequently shared, where elaboration can be offered, disagreements can be aired, and comments can be posted."[4]

3. WHY HAS BLOGGING ATTRACTED SO MUCH ATTENTION?

The media blitz is one reason. Mainstream media (MSM as it's called in the blogosphere) picked up blogs as a story in 2004 and never let go. But underlying the news coverage is a real phenomenon built around three things: scale, speed and impact.

Scale

The explosion in the number of blogs is mind-boggling. When Technorati launched in November 2002, it counted just under 13,000 blogs. Exactly three years later, in November 2005, the online service was tracking over 20 million blogs. The 10 million mark had been celebrated just six months earlier. That's a whole lot of words, pictures, audio files and video clips written, produced and posted by folks from work or home. Naysayers had said that TV-bred couch potatoes would never make the effort to create all this content. They were wrong. And while the first wave of blogs was personal— many written by self-indulgent diarists—the second and third waves have been written by consultants, academics, small business owners and, increasingly, by bigger companies and corporations.

Speed

Blogs are instant and always-on. (By "always-on," I'm referring to the 24/7 nature of the Web. Accessible anytime, anyplace, through any Internet-connected device.) Whether it's a political scandal, a natural disaster or a terrorist attack, people increasingly turn to blogs to get the most up-to-date news and, in turn, to post their version of events. Someone is always listening. We experienced this, live, on September 11, 2001. The major online news sites were overloaded and stopped working. Blogs supplanted mainstream media for on-the-scene reporting, for what was *really happening*. "The need to connect is intense," Donna Hoffman, a Vanderbilt University professor, told the *New York Times*. "While the network TV stations blather, the Internet carries the news and connects the masses in a true interactive sob."[5]

Late that night on 9/11, pioneer blogger and technology entrepreneur Dave Winer wrote: "We got first-hand reports from people who were there . . . real-time human touches that are hard to capture in a print pub with a lead time. There's power in the new communication and development medium we're mastering. Far from being dead, the Web is just getting started."[6] He was referring, of course, to the dot-bomb era that began in 2000 and was in full flower by late 2001.

Turning to Web search is now a reflexive response. If you're frantic with worry about a family member being caught in the path of a hurricane or a tsunami, where do you go online to get more information? A blog, of course. Do a quick Google search by typing in the name of the disaster followed by the word "blog." Choose a blog that looks credible to you. Type in a comment asking the blogger to post the name of your relative. Other readers may see it and pass on a tidbit of information. This underground network of seekers and finders erupted after the Asian tsunami of December 2004 and after Hurricane Katrina, which wreaked havoc on New Orleans and the Gulf Coast in August 2005. Of course, the same instinct to Google applies if you're buying a new car or researching a vacation.

Impact

Blogging began a decade ago as an online outlet for personal musings. Then something happened. Blogs burst into mainstream consciousness in the summer of 2004. Democrat Howard Dean's BlogForAmerica.com, the first-ever official blog for a presidential candidate, helped the candidate raise millions of dollars from online donors during the primary—a first. Hundreds of individual bloggers were granted press credentials at the Democratic and Republican national conventions—a first. By late 2004, it seemed that blogs were beginning to fulfill the promise of the Web as a participatory phenomenon. Now everyone could be a journalist or a reporter (although you weren't guaranteed credibility or readership). Citizen journalism, an emerging concept, was a reality.

4. HOW IS A BLOG DIFFERENT FROM A WEB SITE?

On a practical level, blogs are more engaging than static Web sites. They offer something new to read, view or listen to almost every time you visit. They offer a way to interact online that's easy and quick. It's safe to predict that blogs—or something akin to them—will replace brochurelike home pages.

In the meantime, forward-looking corporate Web sites are including their blog as part of the site's core design and/or including a prominent link from the home page with a bit of enticing copy. Here's the text link one Web design studio used to direct visitors to their blog:

The very best way to get to know us, how we think and what we're passionate about is to read our blog. In addition to offering useful and timely information, it's a fun, entertaining read.

A blog is different from a conventional Web site because it is

- interactive.

- written in a conversational voice.

- created using instant publishing software; usually no tech expertise and no techies or IT staff are required.

- offers an efficient way to alert interested readers every time something new is added—without using email.

- frequently updated, so that it almost always gets higher rankings in search engine results than a static site.

- a form of viral marketing.

As a marketing strategy, blogs are often more effective than traditional Web sites. Blogging is a powerful, low-cost way to get found by the search engines—one of the biggest reasons marketers are paying increasing attention. Prevailing wisdom goes something like this: get found in Internet search results and your voice will count. Be absent online and your company, product or service (unless you're a Fortune 500 brand with a mega marketing budget) practically doesn't exist.

A blog should resonate with the look and feel of your main site. In fact, visitors to your blog page don't even need to know that it's a blog. The blog should be easy to interact with, even for those unfamiliar with blogging's many conventions. Increasingly, entire Web sites are being built on blogging software. This is a low-cost alternative to a pricey content management system (CMS). And often just as effective. Ask your Web consultant about this. If you get a blank stare, hire a new techie.

5. QUICK! WHAT ARE THE THREE MOST IMPORTANT THINGS I NEED TO KNOW ABOUT BLOGGING IN ORDER TO GET STARTED?

1. Companies don't blog; individuals do. That means a corporate blog needs to be written in a human voice. This can be a challenge. It goes against the grain for many companies. Still, if your corporate communications department is responsible for your blog, they can often find an in-house blogger with a lively, distinctive voice. It doesn't have to be your CEO (but it certainly can be; read about CEO bloggers in chapter 5). It might be someone in product development or customer service. He or she doesn't need to wear an official communications hat. You can also hire a blog editor, as Stonyfield Farm, the New Hampshire–based organic yogurt manufacturer, has done. And there are networks of bloggers-for-hire you can tap into.

2. Savvy bloggers read other blogs. Whether or not you choose to launch a blog, you need to be reading blogs. Your employees and/or competitors are most likely already blogging about your industry niche—or possibly your company, products or services. Get used to it. Make use of it. Track what's being said about your company in the blogosphere and you've just discovered next-generation focus groups. It's easy to do. You don't need to hire a market research firm. Although you can: a new breed of market research firms specializing in blog analysis has sprung up. You can use free blog search engines like Blogpulse, Google Blog Search and Technorati. Also, reading other blogs is the best way to dip your toes into the blogosphere and get a feel for what kinds of business blogs are engaging and ring true. And which aren't.

3. Blogging is not a replacement. A blog doesn't replace other forms of on- or offline marketing. But they're fast becoming an adjunct you shouldn't ignore. Blogs are a quick, easy way to communicate and make a connection with your customers and the media. You can still send out press releases, publish an e-newsletter and maintain a corporate Web site. Think of blogs as a low-cost, high-impact add-on to whatever you're doing now to communicate with your key constituencies.

Blogs are a new way to close the gap between you and your customers. And to organize the smart thinking and reams of archived information inside your organization. Finally, blogs are a remarkably effective way to get high search engine rankings. When someone Googles the name of your company or product—or enters keyword phrases that describe what you do—your blog is more apt to come up at the top of the page than your home page. That's because a blog is constantly being refreshed with new content.

Finally, blogs and blogging *are* symptomatic of the next generation of the Web. Web 2.0—as it's being called—is the new participatory Web. It's defined by the abundance of user-generated content—those millions of blog posts, photos, audio and video files, as well as uploaded documents created by users. The new Web is also about real-time collaboration.

6. WHAT MAKES A GOOD CORPORATE BLOG?

It's updated frequently (preferably a couple of times a week). The writing voice is authentic, friendly and conversational. You hear passion and authority (to borrow a phrase from Microsoft's chief employee blogger, Robert Scoble). The writing style has a light touch but it's cogent and grammatically correct. The blog is credible and informative and stays on topic. If you're accepting comments, readers are interacting with the blog by typing in their feedback or questions. Maybe you see trackbacks (links) from other blogs. A good blog serves up a hard-to-quantify mix of information, opinion and controversy. Er, controversy? Yes, even if it just means acknowledging a problem with your product or service. And then listening to the feedback from your readers.

7. WHAT ARE THE LEGAL RISKS OF BLOGGING?

If you boil down the key legal risks of blogging, they fall into two buckets:

- stuff you don't want to reveal (trade secrets, financial information)
- stuff you can get sued for (copyright, libel, privacy issues)[7]

Of course, the lawyers make it more complicated than that. But that's probably what's keeping you up at night if you're worrying about legal liability. You should assume you have employee bloggers, by the way. If you're in a company with 100 or more employees, chances are at least a handful are blogging already.

My advice on the legal front: be aware of the risks—but don't muzzle your bloggers. Instead, work with them to craft corporate blogging guidelines that specifically address the legal issues they should be aware of. It's not that difficult, really. The maxim "be smart" used by Microsoft to guide its bloggers will go a long way. Observing copyright means understanding what fair use is. (As a general rule, never quote more than a few successive paragraphs. If it's a poem, not more than one or two lines.) Refraining from libel or name-calling is common sense and adult behavior. Divulging proprietary or financial information is an obvious no-no.

Companies like Hill & Knowlton, IBM, Intel, Sun Microsystems, Thomas Nelson Publishers and Yahoo have published public blogging guidelines. Your approach to creating guidelines and your requirements will be different depending on whether you are a small private company or a public Fortune 1000. See chapter 3 for some of the finer points to consider. Also consult the Bonus Resources section at the back of the book for examples of blogging policies you can copy from and for legal resources related to blogging.

8. WHAT IF MY EMPLOYEES ARE BLOGGING AND I DON'T KNOW ABOUT IT?

You can find out pretty quickly by doing a Google search on their names or using Google Blog Search. Or just asking. But don't panic. A lot of "real people" (as they say) are blogging these days.

Employee blogging is fast becoming a topic included in employment contracts and employee handbooks. However, in the fall of 2005, close to 70 percent of companies had no blogging guidelines, according to one study.[8] If your organization doesn't have a company-wide blogging policy, take the lead on crafting one. No, don't leave this up to Legal. If you're not blogging yourself, start by consulting with a few blogging colleagues. They'll help you understand blogging etiquette and key questions to consider. Should employees acknowledge their association with your company? Should they offer a disclaimer that views expressed are their own? Can employees blog on company time if theirs is an officially sanctioned blog and part of your company's marketing strategy? (Consult the Bonus Resources section for examples of blogging disclaimers.)

9. HOW DO I GET OVER MY FEAR OF BLOGGING?

First, reassure yourself that it's normal to be a bit nervous about publishing to the Web where anything you write is permanently archived and publicly accessible. It's true that blogging can have unintended consequences—both positive and negative. If your job is to manage and control and package and measure, it's only natural you'll find the uncontrollable aspect of blogs a bit unnerving. Here's what you legitimately can (and should) be worried about:

- employees leaking news of a new product release via their blogs
- employees who are chronic complainers kvetching about what goes on inside your company

- bloggers (they might be your customers?) who take delight in trashing your company, product or service, rightly or wrongly

- Mean-spirited or profane comments left by readers of your company blog (Note: you can easily delete comments. Or review them first and choose not to publish them.)

And on a more personal level, if you're the one who's going to do the blogging, you may be worried about any or all of the following:

- Can I write well enough?

- What will I write about?

- Will I make a fool of myself?

- What if I don't understand blogging etiquette?

- How will I find time to keep the blog updated?

All of the above can be dealt with sensibly. In fact, I devote a whole chapter to confronting fear of blogging (chapter 3) and another on how to write a blog (chapter 7). I hope this book will give you a clear understanding of how the blogosphere works and what other companies are doing. That alone should dispel some of your anxiety.

How else to eliminate the fear factor? Take proactive steps. Start reading a dozen or so blogs on topics you're interested in—either personally or professionally. Type your company or product names into one of the specialized blog search engines and see what comes up. Are you being talked about? If yes, it's time to make the jump into the blogosphere. No? Stay alert. Remember, a blog is nothing more than an interactive Web site. Visitors to your site will increasingly expect to see a blog component on your home page. Don't make this blogging thing more complicated than it needs to be.

10. WHAT KIND OF STAFF / RESOURCES / BUDGET WILL WE NEED TO KEEP A BLOG GOING?

It depends on what kind of blog you launch, how much traffic and interaction you get from readers and what the purpose is. GM's Fast-Lane blog gets hundreds of thousands of page views a month and often hundreds of comments in reaction to a single posting. (Americans care passionately about cars!) If your blog gets this much attention, you're going to need a separate support team to monitor and maintain the blog. It could be one or more people in-house or something you outsource to your PR firm. GM uses their Web agency. The monthly fee for blog maintenance is mixed in with the firm's overall retainer so it's in the range of $5,000 a month. Intuit's Quick-Books Online division appointed a "community manager" to oversee their blog as well as online discussion boards. Stonyfield Farm, the organic yogurt maker, hired a Chief Blogger for $40,000 annually[9] to edit and write the company's blogs.

11. WHO IN MY COMPANY SHOULD BLOG? CAN IT BE MORE THAN ONE PERSON?

Absolutely. If your company has sanctioned—and encourages—employee blogging, you may have dozens, hundreds or thousands of staffers communicating daily through blogs with customers, partners, developers and other stakeholders. IBM, Macromedia, Microsoft and Sun Microsystems are just a few examples of companies who publicly boast about their thousands of employee blogs. It's common for such companies to maintain a public Web page listing all the blogs.[10]

If you've decided to launch an official company blog, you can assemble a group of writers. PR firm Hill & Knowlton created a Collective Conversation blog with multiple authors at blogs.hillandknowlton.com/blogs. A handful of staffers at Clif Bar (the natural energy bar) blog at clifbar.com/blog. They call it the Blah,

Blah, Blog. If your CEO or other top executive isn't the "writing type," you can interview her and create a podcast (downloadable audio file) that you post to your blog. In addition, some creative person on your tech or communications staff can put together a video clip to add to your blog, turning it into a Vlog. You can also hire a professional blogger or blog editor to oversee your company blog. Just don't let someone ghost blog for your CEO. That's a no-no.

12. HOW MUCH TIME DOES IT TAKE TO WRITE AND MAINTAIN A BLOG?

This is my favorite question. I could counter with a Zen-like pronouncement ("How much time does it take to breathe?"). But I won't. Here are a few practical tips on how much time it takes. You might be surprised by the answers. (And see chapter 7 for more writing tips.)

So how much time does it really take on a daily or weekly basis to write and maintain a blog?

- Less time than it takes to put together a professionally designed HTML (i.e., looks like a Web page, not just text) e-newsletter containing multiple articles.

- About as much time as it takes you to skim through your favorite industry news sources and note to yourself what's worth commenting on. In other words, blogging can be an adjunct to keeping up with the news.

- Fewer hours than it takes you or someone in your organization to write a carefully crafted op-ed piece (which may or may not get published).

- The equivalent of half a day a week to write posts for the blog; more time to monitor reader feedback if yours is a highly-trafficked blog like General Motors' FastLane.

- The same amount of time it takes to write emails to multiple colleagues. How many emails do you write to business colleagues in a day?

- Microsoft blogger Robert Scoble's one-word answer: "Starbucks." In other words, if you're connected to the Internet at your local Starbucks, you can be doing something related to blogging. For example, saving tidbits in draft form that you'll come back and publish later to your live blog.

13. HOW DO I CONVINCE SENIOR MANAGEMENT—OR MY BOSS—THAT OUR COMPANY SHOULD BE BLOGGING?

How about this: start by emphasizing the risks of *not* blogging. That will get their attention.

- If you don't blog, you're not part of the conversation in the blogosphere. In other words, bloggers may be saying bad things about your company and if you're not listening to the conversation you have no way to respond quickly and appropriately.

- You're missing out on a fast, efficient communications channel with your customers, the media, investors and other important constituencies.

- If you don't have a blog, your company Web site will soon look, er, so 1990s.

Then make a sensible business case using examples of what other organizations (perhaps your competition) are doing. In broad brush strokes, blogs offer an organization a way to:

- communicate with customers in real-time.

- get positive and negative feedback from key constituencies.

- achieve high search engine rankings without spending a fortune on search engine optimization.

Internal blogs enable your company to capitalize on the enormous amount of knowledge possessed by your employees. They enable real-time and systematic collaboration on software development, product development, sales and other activities. And your kicker: by not blogging you may be hurting your brand. Without a blog as part of your Web site, your company may appear walled off and disinterested in being open to comment and criticism. See chapter 9 for a cheat sheet to make the case to your boss (or employees) for blogging.

14. I'M NOT A TECHIE; HOW MUCH DO I NEED TO KNOW ABOUT THE TECHNICAL FEATURES OF A BLOG?

Not much. Blogging software is really just a user-friendly publishing tool for the Web. If you can send an email, you can compose and publish a blog entry—and update your blog instantly. The software creates date-stamped entries in reverse chronological order, with the most recent appearing at the top of the page. It also does some other neat stuff behind the scenes, such as notifying the blog search engines to tell them you've updated your blog and archiving your entry by date and by category automatically so you, and others, can find it later.

So what makes a blog interactive? Often, a blog includes comments typed in by readers, along with links left by other bloggers (known as trackbacks). These become a permanent part of the blog's content. The technology underlying blogging software is what connects blog to blog. Think of it as a giant snowball that picks up all the connections—between blogger and reader, between blogger and blogger—as it rolls forward. The result? The rapidly expanding blogosphere.

15. I'M A *LITTLE* BIT OF A GEEK: WHAT ARE THE MAIN BLOGGING PLATFORMS AND TOOLS I SHOULD KNOW ABOUT?

The number and type of blog platforms have proliferated over the past several years. The two main categories are hosted (on a blog service) versus non-hosted (in-house). Larger companies generally prefer non-hosted blogging solutions because of privacy and security concerns and to ensure that the blogging platform integrates seamlessly with whatever software system is powering their corporate directory, email, etc. A new generation of corporate blogging platforms is also emerging. (See chapter 8 for more information.)

RSS (also referred to as a Web feed) stands for Really Simple Syndication. It is an essential feature of a blog. An RSS feed enables readers to subscribe to a blog via an RSS newsreader such as NewsGator, Bloglines or NetNewsWire (for Mac) and get automatic updates whenever new content is added. The benefit is that no email is involved, so the updates are not blocked by spam filters or lost in a clogged inbox. Users also like the privacy of not submitting an email address in order to subscribe. See the glossary for a more technical definition of RSS.

16. WHAT WRITING STYLE WORKS FOR A CORPORATE BLOG?

In a word, non-corporate. A human voice. The voice of an individual who is passionate and authoritative about the topic at hand. A good company blog sounds like it's written by one person (or a small group with each blogger being identified by name). An effective blog post is what überblogger Doc Searls calls "an email to everyone." The blog is not written in corporate-speak, nor as a dry memo or press release.

Here's an example of the sleeves-rolled-up voice of a good corporate

blogger. Sun Microsystems COO Jonathan Schwartz blogs at blogs.
sun.com/jonathan. In June 2005 he wrote:

> One of the big upsides of my job is hobnobbing. I clearly
> didn't check with our corporate communications team before
> saying that, but let's be honest—it's cool to sit with a head of
> state, or a head of a corporation, or a CIO with an IT depart-
> ment bigger than Sun's entire employee base.

Kind of fun to get an inside glimpse of what a Fortune 500 executive is thinking, isn't it?

17. SO WHO'S BLOGGING IN THE FORTUNE 500?

Only a handful of these mega companies, so far. In fact, just 24 (less
than 5 percent of) Fortune 500 corporations as of March 2006, according to the Fortune 500 Business Blogging Index. This online resource is a wiki (a group-edited Web page) that you can visit and
add information to at: www.socialtext.net/bizblogs/index.cgi. Also
see the accompanying book blog at TheCorporateBloggingBook.
com for easy access to these and other links. The number of Fortune
500 blogs will undoubtedly be higher by the time you visit the Fortune 500 blogging wiki.[11]
  Note that the best Fortune 500 blogs tend to be authored by one
or more high-profile executives, not by corporate communications.
(Google's official blog is an exception. More on that in chapter 4.
Google was just shy of the Fortune 500 list at this writing.) In
addition, thousands of midlevel employees at IBM, Microsoft and
Sun Microsystem write independent but officially sanctioned blogs.
Some say these voices from the trenches are more effective at putting
a face on a mega corporation. The best example is the prolific,
friendly and authoritative Robert Scoble, known as Microsoft's chief
blogger. Robert, whose official title is "technical evangelist" (go figure), is consistently listed on any Top 100 list of best-read blogs.

You can visit his blog at scobleizer.wordpress.com for one of the best examples of how to do it right.

A partial list of Fortune 500 corporate blogs as of press time:

- Amazon Web Services Blog at aws.typepad.com

- Boeing's blog written by VP Marketing Randy Baseler at boeing.com/randy

- Cisco's High Tech Policy group blog at cisco.com/gov/blog

- Cox Communications' Digital Straight Talk ("Your inside guide to broadband communications") at digitalstraighttalk.com

- EDS's Next Big Thing blog at eds.com/sites/cs/blogs/eds_next_big_thing_blog/default.aspx.

- General Motors' FastLane blog written by GM vice chairman Bob Lutz and other senior execs at fastlane.gmblogs.com

- Hewlett-Packard's executive and technical blogs at www.hp.com/go/blogs

- Sprint's Things That Make You Go Wireless at businessblog.sprint.com/1/1

- Sun Microsystems' COO Jonathan Schwartz's blog at blogs.sun.com/jonathan

- Texas Instruments' Video 360 blog at blogs.ti.com

- Xerox's Palo Alto Research Center PlayOn blog (exploring the social dimensions of virtual worlds) at blogs.parc.com/playon

18. WHAT ABOUT EXAMPLES OF EFFECTIVE BLOGS BY SMALL AND MEDIUM-SIZED COMPANIES OR ORGANIZATIONS?

Selecting only a few is hard, as there are thousands of blogs in this category. But here are some good examples. I chose them because they are particularly well written and engaging. They range from one-person shops to large trade associations. Again, find these links (and additional examples) at TheCorporateBloggingBook.com.

- Air Conditioning Contractors of America (ACCABuzz) at acca.blogs.com

- Designwear e-tailer Bluefly.com at flypaper.bluefly.com

- English Cut (Savile Row tailor Thomas Mahon) at englishcut.com

- Seth Godin's blog at sethgodin.typepad.com

- Indium Corp.'s Dr. Lasky's blog at indium.com/drlasky

- Intuit QuickBooks blogs at quickbooksgroup.com/webx/blogs

- Lincoln Sign Company's JD Iles at signsneversleep.typepad.com

- National Association of Manufacturers at blog.nam.org/pat-cleary.php

- Steve Spangler Science at stevespangler.com

- Stonyfield Farm at stonyfield.com/weblog

19. WHAT ARE SOME GOOD CEO BLOGS?

These are growing in number and often consistently smart. Makes sense, doesn't it? Top executives often get there because they're incisive thinkers. As one CEO blogger—Zane Safrit, of Conference Calls Unlimited—put it: "Blogging helps me articulate and refine ideas in a linear fashion . . . ideas I may be thinking about for our company. So blogging improves my ability to communicate with my employees." (zane.typepad.com/ccuceo)

This list goes a long way, on its own, toward answering the question: Should the CEO, or senior executive, blog? (One caveat: it helps if the CEO likes to write and possesses some blogging DNA.) I've chosen the following list because these folks really "get" blogging. I've omitted Boeing's Randy Baseler, GM's Bob Lutz and Sun Microsystems' Jonathan Schwartz because they are mentioned above as examples of Fortune 500 blogs.

- Matt Blumberg (ReturnPath) at onlyonce.blogs.com

- Karen Christensen (Berkshire Publishing Group) at berkshirepublishing.com/blog

- Mark Cuban (Dallas Mavericks) at blogmaverick.com

- Richard Edelman (Edelman PR) at edelman.com/speak_up/blog

- Michael Hyatt (Thomas Nelson Publishers) at michaelhyatt.blogs.com/fromwhereisit

- Alan Meckler (Jupitermedia) at weblogs.jupitermedia.com/meckler

- Bob Parsons (Go Daddy) at bobparsons.com

- Dave Sifry (Technorati) at sifry.com/alerts

- Fred Wilson (Union Square Ventures) at avc.blogs.com

- Irving Wladawsky-Berger (IBM) at irvingwb.typepad.com

See chapter 5 for more on CEO bloggers.

20. SO REALLY, WHAT'S THE POINT?

Fair question. Because, in truth, creating and maintaining a blog takes work. It requires real thinking, good writing, the right touch and persistence. In addition, the ROI isn't precisely quantifiable. And there are legitimate legal issues that need to be thought about ahead of time and conveyed to executive and employee bloggers. Here's a three-part answer:

Blog or be blogged.   Either you join the conversation in the blogosphere or you're deaf to it. If you choose the latter, you've lost control. You can't respond to what's being said about you; you can't proactively initiate conversations. You'll look like you're clueless and/or stonewalling. If you choose the former, you can shape what's being said about your company even if you can't entirely control it.

Think of blogging as a three-legged stool.   The legs are the search engines, your customers and the media. If you've got a blog, you'll rank high in search engine results. If you've got a blog, you're taking advantage of a remarkably low-cost way to communicate with—and get feedback from—your customers. Finally, if your company is blogging you will likely attract media interest. It's still early days in blogdom. Be the first in your niche and you'll be noticed. If you're a Fortune 1000 company with a recognizable name, you'll get calls from reporters without having to use your PR agency.

Blogs are part of next-generation Web sites.   They are the real-time, interactive part of a site. They may not be known as blogs in the future. They may evolve into something bloglike that enables reader participation with your site and with your company. But if you don't embrace blogs now—or at least start thinking about incorporating a blog into your site—then you're stuck in the old, static Web. Can you afford that? Online search is driving business results these days, whether you're a local business or a mega corporation. You want to be found. You want your online presence to be memorable. Don't get left behind.

CHAPTER 2

A Quick Romp Through the Corporate Blogosphere

"It would be cool to have an online journal, so here it is."
July 24, 2001
—First blog posting by Wil Wheaton,
child actor turned blogger and author.[1]

A BIT OF EVOLUTION

For a long time, cool was the operative word when you entered the blogosphere. As in, "You've got a blog? Hey, *cool!*" In early 1999, it was a given that you were a techie if you were blogging. Only several dozen blogs—called Weblogs—existed.[2] These distinctive Web sites, lists of links along with sparse commentary, were hand-coded and maintained by Web designers or programmers in their spare time. Blogging was a *new* new thing known only to a handful of Web geeks.

Then in August 1999, along came Blogger.com, a free blogging service. And everything changed. Now anybody could start a blog in minutes. Overnight it seemed, the number of blogs jumped from dozens to thousands. And a pecking order emerged. The authors of the first A-list blogs—the ones that those-in-the-know linked to and paid attention to—really *were* cool. They set a kind of standard for sharp thinking, articulate writing and strong personality that have come to define good blogging.

A small sampling: Doc Searls, a technology geek and one of the coauthors of *The Cluetrain Manifesto*, started blogging at doc.weblogs.com in 1999. You'll still find him there, posting new entries several times a day about what he calls "the continuing end of Business as Usual." *Cluetrain*, published in 2000, remains the seminal book to define markets as "conversations" and to posit that consumers want businesses to speak to them in a human voice. Joi Ito, an Internet technology entrepreneur who divides his time between Japan and the U.S., started blogging in 1993. You'll find a record of his life, complete with photos and writing at joi.ito.com.[3] Halley Suitt, a former dot-com executive turned writer, has blogged at halleyscomment.blogspot.com since 2002. In her words, Halley's Comment is a "sexy single mom's blog about business, politics, alpha males, dating, kids, divorce and life in Boston." (Be sure to visit. Her deft writing combines the personal with the professional in flawless blog style.) Halley is also the author of the first *Harvard Business Review* case study about business blogging.[4]

"Blog: I like that it's roughly onomatopoeic of vomiting. These sites (mine included!) tend to be a kind of information upchucking."

> —*Peter Merholz, who coined the term "blog" in 1999 as a contraction of "Web" and "log"*

Between 2002 and 2005, the number of blogs skyrocketed from thousands to millions. The idea of an online journal was intoxicating. And it wasn't just an outlet for teenage angst. Suddenly, confessional writing was accepted, easy to publish—and, hey, everyone was doing it! Bloggers were sharing their opinions on everything from parenting to trademark law (lawyers love to blog; they've even got their own category called blawgs). Blogs mushroomed to cover tiny niches on every conceivable topic. Oh, and of course politics. And not just U.S. politics. Bloggers began reporting from war-torn Iraq and from repressive regimes around the world. Visit Global Voices Online at cyber.law.harvard.edu/globalvoices to get a sense of the conversations taking place from Afghanistan to Zimbabwe.

What's more, a blog wasn't just a place to comment on the world around you, it was a place to publish your day-to-day life, your world. A blog was your online identity and for some, a more significant identity than your offline self. What's interesting is that this notion of blog as 360-degree "me" hasn't gone away. If anything, it's evolved into a form of social networking engaged in by everyone under the age of 30 (or is it 40?) through free online services like Yahoo! 360, MySpace and for the college crowd, Facebook.

More recently, the 360-degree concept has come to define the next generation of blogging tools, used both by individuals and by large companies. By specifying different permission or access levels you can enable selected users to see only certain sections of your blog.

FROM PERSONAL DIARY TO CORPORATE COMMUNICATIONS VEHICLE

So if blogs were highly personal—and often self-indulgent—personal diaries, how in heck did this phenomenon cross over into the *business* world? It's worth taking a moment to ponder. It will defuse the notion that "corporate blogging" is an oxymoron. (This was a running joke in the blogosphere for a while.) If blogs are personal, then how can corporations blog? And it will also begin to explain why blogging is a pervasive phenomenon—one that businesses can adapt—that isn't going away anytime soon.

First, for the thousands of techies and entrepreneurs immersed in the dot-com boom, the line between personal and professional was blurred. Twenty-hour days, frantic sprints to release version 1.0 and too much caffeine meant that whatever living you were doing was happening right then, *right now.* What did it matter if you were thinking about last night's date while writing this morning's code. It all flowed together. And anyone interested in your thoughts would certainly understand.

Second, the Internet itself is increasingly accessible, through wifi and other devices, including cell phones. Customers—possibly yours—are plugged in for several hours a day or more. Blogs, as a marketing and communications channel, thrive in this always-on ecosystem. Smart companies are picking up on this. If you're one of them you know that nobody likes to be sold to (the premise of traditional advertising). But almost everybody wants to read about, converse with, listen to or otherwise interact with useful or entertaining information about stuff—or an issue—they care about. (Good blogs are both useful *and* entertaining.)

Third, the blogosphere has proven to be a surprisingly persistent phenomenon. Blogging took off after Sept. 11, 2001. When email didn't work, blogs often did. That day blurred all boundaries, from personal to political, from local to global. We got used to personal accounts of the disaster turning into discussions of privacy versus national security. It's a short hop from public debate of political issues to broader business themes.

Another reason for the crossover from personal to business was that mainstream media began treating corporate blogging as news. One afternoon in the spring of 2005 I entered the phrase "corporate blogging" into the search service that is part of Google News. I was asking Google to do a continuous search on that phrase and alert me by email every time "corporate blogging" appeared in a news story. At first I got an alert once a week or so. But by mid-2005, links to articles with that phrase in it were coming once or twice a day.

A typical story: on May 13, 2005, Tom Foremski breathlessly headlined an article in the blog-style publication SiliconValleyWatcher. com: "Can blogging boost IBM's revenues and reduce layoffs?"

What happened to this sexy-sounding headline gives you an insider's peek at how the blogosphere works. You can still see it if you type siliconvalleywatcher.com/mt/archives/2005/05/scoop_can_blogg.php into your browser. But this is now an orphan Web page, not part of the Silicon Valley Watcher's permanent archive. After IBM's vice president of communications, Jim Finn, complained that the headline tying blogging to revenues was inaccurate, Foremski updated the blog article with the less exciting title: "IBM is preparing to launch a massive corporate wide blogging initiative as it seeks to extend its expertise online." Reporter Foremski made the "links" between blogging, sales and IBM's public layoffs, Finn told me in an interview. "Not us." The takeaway: you can make changes to blog entries, but the original words live forever in a kind of Web page snapshot!

So what do corporate blogs accomplish? They're rarely as edgy and cool as blogs written by savvy Net watchers. What's the point? The easiest way to answer these questions is to give you a guided tour. Let's start with a broad brushstroke to divide corporate blogs into two main categories: internal (behind a firewall) and external (accessible to anyone with a Web browser).

INTERNAL BLOGS: THE FIRST SILENT WAVE

Internal blogs are not an entirely different species from public-facing ones. Just substitute the word "employee" for "customer" and you can use them in much the same way. The key difference is that inward-facing blogs are meant only for internal consumption. They're behind a firewall, sometimes built into a company's intranet and not accessible through a public URL. They are authored by employees and/or managers. They may also be written by the CEO or a senior executive to communicate with the troops.

In fact, internal blogs—for improved collaboration and communication—are the first, largely silent wave of corporate blogging. Whatever your interest in blogging, internal blogs are what many companies start with. In fact, that's the first piece of advice you'll hear from any blogging expert: if you want to blog publicly, start internally. Experiment with subject matter, who's doing the writing, frequency and so forth. Get up to speed, then tear down the firewall and give the public access if that makes sense for the topic of your blog.

While blog search engines are tracking the exploding number of public blogs, no one can say for sure how many corporations are running internal blogs. Thousands is a safe number. It only makes sense. Blogging software can be adapted to mesh seamlessly with enterprise intranets. From "permissions" (who has authority to access what) to searchability to editorial review and versioning (saving each iteration), every feature of a blog can be adapted to internal systems already in place.

The early pioneers of internal blogging have used them for project management, for more efficient communications and for knowledge sharing. They range from manufacturing companies, banks and airlines to publishers, universities and Internet companies. And last but not least, IBM. The e-business giant began using internal blogs in 2003. Close to 20,000 of IBM's 300,000-plus employees worldwide had registered on the company's internal Blog Central by the end of 2005, IBM blogger-in-chief Christopher Barger told me.

Knowledge Sharing: Disseminating Tips, Expertise and Even Negative Feedback

The most notable thing about internal blogs is that they're a user-friendly way to systematically categorize—and retrieve—the extraordinary amount of knowledge that lies untapped inside most large corporations. Some say that internal blogs represent a revolution in how companies are handling knowledge management. Two-thirds of the companies responding to a survey by the Economist Intelligence Unit reported that executives "currently feel unable to exploit large amounts of corporate information." In other words, while their IT departments generate lots of data, they can't filter or analyze it.[5]

The flip side is that internal blogs can capture knowledge from lower-level employees and send it *up,* by making it easily accessible. As the Intranet Journal put it: "Existing communication channels within companies tend to come from on high, be nicely polished, highly wordsmithed by many including the lawyers, and distributed to the masses. With a blog, the power of communication is given to individuals at much lower ranks within the organization."[6]

Googling Googlers

In addition to a number of well-publicized public blogs, Web services giant Google runs several hundred blogs internally. Every new employee is given a blog account on BIG (Blogger Inside Google). But only a fraction of Google's 5,000 employees are regular bloggers, according to David Krane, Google's VP of corporate communications. The internal blogs are used primarily for project status reports and for "fun and musings," he told me. One internal blog is called Google Love Notes. It's used by customer service reps to post thank-you notes from users who've found long lost family or friends (or high school flames) through Google search.[7]

More Efficient Project Management

Stanford University uses a blogging intranet to enable different departments to exchange information more efficiently. And MIT's Sloan School of Management uses internal "blog forums."[8] Project heads act as the blog publishers. Team members contribute "comments" as appropriate. The internal blogs enable cross communication between projects as well as quicker top-down review. According to Sloan School CIO Al Essa, face-to-face meetings are now much more productive. They're no longer spent in project-review mode. Participants now talk about what's next rather than boring everyone with a recitation of what's happened to date.

Information Sharing

Like many institutions, German investment bank Dresdner Kleinwort Wasserstein wasn't comfortable with the idea of external blogs. So the bank set up over 120 internal blogs for information sharing.

Some are being used to streamline communications about the company's IT system—and thus reduce all those annoying emails about server downtime. Other blogs are being used by the bank's traders as a way to share tips, insights and research. The twist is that users are encouraged to offer ideas, to make requests and even to be constructively critical of policies or procedures. "We think of it as the open-source marketplace for ideas," says the bank's CIO, JP Rangaswami. "It lets us expose concepts or issues to a wide audience and discuss them dispassionately."[9]

Blogs as Email Killer

Technology magazine publisher Ziff Davis Media reduced group emails from 100 a day to zero after installing an internal blogging platform. The goal initially was strategic planning. The company wanted to consolidate the online versions of several of its leading publications. But actual use quickly evolved into something else— the task-specific coordination of a 50-person team to launch a new product. In addition to a dramatic reduction in email volume, Ziff Davis figured soft cost savings to be more than $1 million (computed on an annual basis). What was projected to be a four-month project was finished in three.[10]

> *"We used to have over 100 group emails per day. Now it's rarely one per week, we've saved a month in a four-month software project, and everyone is on the same page."*
> —*Tom Jessiman, Ziff Davis*
> *general manager*

By the way, a key point when it comes to internal blogs is that companies may not be calling them that. They're next-generation collaboration and content management tools. And employees may not even know that they're blogging. See the sidebar with a list of practical ways to use an internal blog.

What to Do with Your Internal Blog

From communications and technology expert Shel Holtz, here's a list of ways you can use an internal blog:[11]

- **Alerts**—Don't you hate getting those emails that let you know when the server's going to be down? People who need to know can subscribe to [the] server status Weblog. Instead of having to send out those emails, IT can simply request that employees subscribe to their blog.

- **Projects**—Companies have terrible institutional memories when it comes to projects. Anybody who needs to delve into a project's records to find out how a decision was reached a year ago is probably out of luck. Project teams can set up a group blog to maintain an ongoing record of decisions and actions. Project leaders can also maintain a blog to announce to the rest of the company the current status of the project.

- **Departmental**—Departments can maintain blogs to let the rest of the company know of current offerings or achievements. Imagine the marketing department being able to submit a simple post to its own blog announcing the availability of new marketing brochures or other collateral.

- **News**—Employees can contribute industry or company news to a group blog, or cover news they have learned in their own personal blogs.

- **Brainstorming**—Employees in a department or on a team can brainstorm about strategy, process and other topics.

- **Customers**—Employees can share the substance of customer visits or phone calls.

- **Personal blogs**—Even though this sounds like a time-waster, a personal blog can prove valuable in the organization. Consider an engineer who reads a lot and attends meetings of his professional association. He updates his blog with summaries of the articles he's read in journals (with links to the journal's Web site) and notes he took at the meeting. Employees who find value in this information will read the blog; those who don't care—anybody who isn't an engineer, perhaps—aren't missing anything if they don't. And if he posts an article or two that have nothing to do with work, well, who said work can never be fun?

- **CEO blog**—What a great way for the CEO to get closer to employees. Imagine a new CEO hosting a blog called "My First Hundred Days" in which he writes daily about his experiences and lets employees comment in order to help him get acclimated.

Blogging as Part of IBM's Communications Kit

As soon as you log in to IBM's blog "dashboard" on the company's intranet, according to Philippe Borremans, IBM's PR manager for Belgium and Luxembourg, you see an overview of all the most recent activity. This includes all blog entries along with comments left by blog readers. Essentially the blogs function as internal, *searchable* diaries. They're used for everything from personal journals to project management, for knowledge sharing between teams or to focus on a particular topic like public relations, Borremans told me. Anyone who hops onto a project can quickly get up to speed without having to reinvent the wheel.

But with a range of collaboration tools available, less than half of IBM's internal blogs are maintained, he said. Wikis (group-edited Web pages) and Instant Messaging (IM) are just as popular. "If I need a quick answer I'll use instant messaging or chat," Borremans said. "If it's a bit more complicated I will phone. If I need a written response I'll send an email. But if I find some interesting material I'll post it on a blog. And if it's information to be reused (like a document template) I'll put it on a wiki."[12]

Borremans's pragmatic and non-starry-eyed approach to blogs is the norm when it comes to internal blogs. They're not cool; they're just a tool.

An Internal Blog for Invitees Only

One company that's tried something a little different with a non-public blog is Daimler-Chrysler. The company set up a by-invitation-only blog for the media. Jason Vines, Chrysler Group's longtime head of communications, along with veteran journalist Ed Garsten, the blog's editorial director, write the entries. It offers them a way to get the backstory about company and auto industry events out to reporters. Garsten told me: "Vines is a bit of a legend in the Motor City. Reporters love him for his accessibility, humor and skill as a communicator. Jason wanted to set up a blog open only to journalists where he could engage them in a little give and take in a sort of safe haven, which is why TheFirehouse.biz is closed."

The blog was roundly criticized by some business blogging observers when it launched in the fall of 2005 for not being "open" to the public. Responded Garsten: "We realize the idea of a 'closed' blog is counter to prevailing thought in the blogosphere. But blogging is still an evolving medium that different constituencies will begin to use in ways that make sense to them. We're not about exclusivity or secretness. We are about communicating with a certain subset of people and aiming our content toward them."[13]

The blog seems to work well in that regard. As a lead up to January's annual auto show in Detroit the blog was featuring podcasts (downloadable audio interviews) with Chrysler executives. Garsten explained in a late December entry: "Broadcasters and Webcasters are encouraged to pull sound bites from the podcasts and we will provide written transcripts of the executive interviews to make it easier for print journalists to pull quotes." (Garsten let me in for a look-see when the blog launched. I logged back in several months later for this update.)

Again, practicality rules on an internal blog. External blogs—the second destination on our walking tour—on the other hand, can be used more creatively.

EXTERNAL BLOGS: THE SECOND WAVE

The big idea behind corporate blogs is that they can do a number of things that weren't previously possible on a large scale, on a small budget and in (almost) real-time. External blogs are:

- an informal way to publish company news.

- a place to *solicit* feedback from customers and prospects about a new product or service.

- a channel to build up the expertise and "thought leadership" of your company.

- another place to publish bits and pieces of useful information that don't make it into your e-newsletter or print publications.

- a new breed of marketing collateral, much like a downloadable white paper, which you use as one hook in your sales process.

Employee Versus Corporate Blogs

I want to draw your attention to one other division in corporate blogging—the distinction between employee-written blogs and official company blogs. Blogging purists will tell you that the voice of an employee from deep within a large company is apt to be more authentic. Whereas a corporate blog—or even a top executive blog—tends to spout the party line. Chris Anderson, author of *The Long Tail: Why the Future Is Selling Less of More* (Hyperion, 2006) opined on his blog:

> It's a huge mistake to equate executive blogs with business blogging . . . The best business blogs come from the employees, not the bosses. They have more time, and are less prone to marketing gobbledygook and gnomic platitudes. And those kind of blogs are on the rise, not the decline.

I'll let you decide for yourself. Yes, many midlevel employee blogs are hugely entertaining as well as revealing. One of my favorites is Microsoft recruiter Heather Hamilton's blog at blogs. msdn.com/heatherleigh. It's filled with intriguing tidbits about how to get hired by the software giant in a marketing or finance position. As well as her personal thoughts. Of course, the reason she feels free to speak her mind is that Microsoft sanctions employee blogs. That requires giving up central command and control of the message—and many organizations aren't ready to do that.

It's interesting to note that those companies that encourage employee blogging are creating the kind of open corporate culture that does in fact breed honest and interesting communication from the trenches. So there you have a bit of a paradox, perhaps. Companies with more employee bloggers (Microsoft has several thousand) may have fewer senior executive blogs. And vice versa.

As with almost everything in blogging, there are as many exceptions as there are rules. In fact, forget the rules. Perhaps the biggest mistake you can make is to make *any* firm pronouncements about what works—or what doesn't—in corporate blogging. We're still in early innings. Corporate blogging only came to mainstream attention in 2005. I think it's too soon to lay down the law for what you can or can't do as a corporate blogger. We're all making this up as we go along.

Still, without sounding too draconian, you've got to abide by basic blogging etiquette no matter who in your company is going to blog:

- Write with a human voice (no corporate-speak allowed).

- Post frequently (at least once a week, preferably more often).

- Be transparent about who is writing the blog and what the purpose is.

- Create a conversation with your readers (blogging is not a monologue).

- Link to useful resources outside your Web site, etc.

Before we get into the mechanics of how to do that, let's confront fear of blogging.

CHAPTER 3

Confronting Fear of Blogging

"(Blogs) are the ultimate vehicle for brand-bashing,
personal attacks, political extremism
and smear campaigns."
—*Forbes* magazine article,
"Attack of the Blogs"[1]

When it comes to corporate blogging, the elephant in the room is fear. Feel free to come right out and say it: this blogging thing sounds scary. *Forbes* magazine focused on the fear in a November 2005 cover story, "Attack of the Blogs." The article did point out some legitimate dangers: namely, there do exist a small sliver of bloggers who deliberately spread untruths ("an online lynch mob," *Forbes* called them[2]). These lowlifes tend to be more visible online where they can spout invective and easily publish a permanent record of dreck. But the number of bloggers out of millions who fit into this category is tiny.

So while your fears of the wild woolly blogosphere may be founded, the reality is that there are some straightforward strategies to keep them in check. Still, the notion persists that the freewheeling nature of blogging doesn't fit with corporate culture. If you're a "suit" and fear is your number one response when you hear the phrase corporate blogging, you're not alone. There are legitimate legal concerns, PR concerns, time concerns. Here's a chart showing the major fears—and possible solutions.

Fear	Fact as Antidote
Time	Not as much as you think
Legal liability	Set up Corporate Blogging Guidelines and use common sense
Employees wasting time on blogs	Blogging is more efficient than group emails
Getting bitten by the blogosphere	Follow Blogging Guidelines and read other blogs to learn the etiquette
Damaging your brand by allowing negative comments	Review comments in advance but still allow negative feedback; they make you more credible
Writing	Choose your blogging topic wisely; learn how to slice and dice it over time
Not getting any business results	ROB (return on blogging) is a new concept but it can be measured
Managing the technical aspects of a blog	Blogging software is easy to master, even for the non-techie
Losing control	Get over it

I'll elaborate on fears related to ROI, writing and tools and technology in chapters 6, 7 and 8. In the meantime, let's confront the biggest fear: *fear of losing control.*

You may be thinking: what happens if something controversial or negative comes up and you want to control the message but it gets *out there* in the blogosphere and bloggers—perhaps your own employees?—run wild with it. The *Forbes* cover story may not have been entirely accurate (it was widely regarded as skewed and scaremongering) but it tapped into a mother lode of anxiety. The biggest fear is "some sort of backlash," Forrester analyst Charlene Li told me.[3] Companies are afraid that employee bloggers "will say something inappropriate, embarrassing or even illegal." The other major fear is that readers of a corporate blog will "post negative comments about your company, product or service," she said.

It turns out that both of these fears—employee bloggers and fear of criticism—can be dealt with sensibly. But not just by creating blogging guidelines and policies. It requires a certain state of mind to be able to tolerate negative feedback. As Gary Grates, former chief of corporate communications for General Motors North America, put it, blogging "is about hearing the cold, hard truth about your business. If you don't have a strong self-awareness of how you're perceived, you're history. The dose of reality has been particularly instructive for us. There are a lot of things we're not trying to defend." He was referring, of course, to the criticism of GM's bland car designs as well as the beef that the automaker has continued to turn out big, gas-guzzling models. "Corporate vanity," he told me, "is the biggest problem."[4]

Concern about your corporate image certainly applies if you're an executive worried about lawsuits and/or losing control of "the message." If you're an employee, you're probably thinking about something else. The unspoken, just-below-the-surface feeling that workers in big—and small—companies have on a day-to-day basis. Fear of speaking up in a meeting, fear of saying the wrong thing, fear of confronting your boss. Fear, in short, of *getting fired.*

Well, get over it. It's not a good reason to avoid blogging. Your job isn't secure anyway. Close to 400,000 private-sector jobs were lost in the first four years of George W. Bush's presidency. Corporate America isn't the safe haven for loyal employees it once was. Sorry if

I sound prickly, but staring down some of these fears is what makes the blogosphere go round. You have to be just the teensiest bit of a renegade in order to buy into blogging. You have to be willing to try something new and to tolerate some uncertainty. To be an innovator, in a word. Blogging is part of the new wave of technologies that is transforming the Internet into, well, a more user-friendly place.

Are You Afraid to Blog?

By Robert Scoble, Microsoft's chief blogger

I meet a lot of people around the industry. Almost every time I meet someone, I ask them "do you have a Weblog?" That's my way of saying "I like you and want to hear more of your ideas." Even deeper: I want a permanent relationship with you (and not of the sexual kind, either).

I've asked this question of people at Apple. Google. IBM. eBay. Real Networks. Cisco. Intel. HP. Amazon. And, yes, here at Microsoft.

Too often the answer is "I couldn't do that." "Why not?" I ask.

"Because I might get fired," is often the answer. I hate that answer. It's an example of corporate fear. An artifact of a management system that doesn't empower its employees to act on behalf of customers.

I find this fear disturbing. Imagine being a flight attendant with this kind of fear. "Sorry, I can't talk to the passengers in this plane today cause I might get fired."[5]

TIME: THE TOP FEAR FACTOR

Both corporate managers and small business owners have repeatedly told me that "too much time" is their chief concern about blogging. They're worried about the hours it will take to create content for a blog, to keep it updated, to come up with fresh and interesting ideas. Sixty-five percent of the 708 marketers who responded to a survey I conducted in 2005 cited "the time it would take to write" as their most important concern about maintaining a blog.[6] Fifty-one percent worried what to write about. In another study, Web agency Backbone Media identified the same concern about time—calling it "cost in terms of man hours"—as the chief roadblock to blogging.[7]

Yeah, it does take time. Blogging burnout is a real phenomenon. *Wired* magazine wrote about it as early as 2004, noting, "While they enjoy what they're doing, many [bloggers] find that keeping up with the pressures to post regularly and to be sharp, witty and incisive is often too much."[8] It's the flip side of success. If your blog develops a regular following your readers are waiting for your next post. As Markos Moulitsas Zuniga, author of the hugely popular anti-Bush blog, Daily Kos, put it, "There's always pressure to have new content up on the site . . . You can sense it when you post something new and 10 minutes later there's 50 comments. You can almost feel they [the readers] were sitting there waiting."[9]

The same is true for the more conservative political blog, Instapundit, written by University of Tennessee law professor Glenn Reynolds. If he stops posting for a day or even a few hours, he has said, readers email him to find out if he's OK. Of course, that immediacy and connection with your readers is what all the excitement is about. It's "real" communication, as opposed to canned corporate-speak. And of course it's what fuels the writing of many bloggers—the prospect of enthusiastic and involved readers.

Note however that the Daily Kos is a *publication* supported by advertising and as such is expected to keep, well, publishing. A corporate blog, generally, is a communications vehicle that happens to *look like* a publication. If you want to flout a blogging "best practice," and publish less frequently, go right ahead. Corporate blogging occupies its own corner of the blogosphere. If you're a pioneer, as many of the companies I profile are, then you get to help make the rules.

A blog published on a company Web site is going to have a team or at least several people behind it. These folks may be allied with your Web content staff or your communications team or your marketing department. But it's most likely going to be more than one person in a bigger organization. In addition, you're going to have a content strategy, both for creating the blog and for keeping it going. Yes, you'll try for passion and spontaneity in your blog. But it will be planned. And that's OK.

"I've never really found the time to blog, so to speak. For me blogging isn't about sitting down on a regular basis and dreaming up something to say. It's more about indignation, frustration, pride and beliefs. I always have my BlackBerry with me. When I'm feeling inspired I jot something down. I've always been this way."

—Bob Lutz, General Motors[10]

Another time concern about blogging is that it's a distraction to employees. According to an analysis by *Advertising Age*, U.S. workers annually are wasting the equivalent of 551,000 years reading blogs. AdAge.com calculated that 35 million workers (one in four) visited blogs in 2005 and spent 3.5 hours or 9 percent of the work week reading them.[11]

But the same concern could be expressed about employees spending too much time on email or surfing the Web. And blogs are, of course, just Web sites. So where do you draw the line? How do you separate blogging—reading or writing them—from the other forms of online communication and information gathering that are part of every knowledge worker's modus operandi?

You don't. Blogging can and should be lumped in with email, Instant Messaging, chat rooms, discussion boards, forums—in other words, the kinds of online communications your employees are already engaged in.

CREATING CORPORATE BLOGGING GUIDELINES

"If you're not having conversations with your employees about the ramifications of all these means of communication, including podcasts, talking to the media on their own and talking to their friends," said intellectual property attorney Denise Howell, a pioneer blogger herself, then you've got a problem. "There are so many ways your employees can talk about what your business is doing . . . Blogging is just another way of having a social interaction but it's more durable."[12]

The point, she said, is "to get ahead of the fear curve" and tell your employees *how* you want them to converse about your company. Dryly written policies and procedures manuals or employee handbooks are not the way to pass on this kind of information, Denise advised. "It's more effective to have discussions and training and hash through these issues in a blood and guts kind of way to arrive at a consensus." And essential, she said, to have a broad communications policy "that folds in blogging, IM (Instant Messaging) and other forms of durable communication."

According to a survey by PR firm Edelman, 70 percent of companies did not have a blogging policy, per se, in 2005.[13] A handful of technology companies like Sun Microsystems have had Internet communications guidelines in place for years, presumably because they understand the ramifications of public—and hence findable—online writing. But most companies are still scrambling to make sense of blogging in the context of business. "There are no hard and fast rules about what a corporation should do when it comes to blogging," employment attorney Mara Levin told me.[14] When we spoke, she had recently crafted blogging guidelines for several of her clients, all private companies. Her guidelines cover points such as:

- Do not defame or discuss your colleagues and their behavior.

- Do not write anything defamatory.

- Do not blog on company time.

- Identify your blog as a personal blog and state that the views are your own (i.e., include a disclaimer).

- Do not reveal confidential info.

- Do not reveal trade secrets.

Smaller companies are more neurotic about negative comments, she said, so sometimes she adds the provision: "Do not say anything disparaging about your employer." (Often, higher-level employees have separate confidentiality and non-compete agreements, which cover what they can or can't talk about, even on a blog.) Smaller private companies tend to have simpler policies, she said. The point of their guidelines is usually "to protect the company's rights and to provide an adequate basis for firing an employee." Translated, you *can* get fired for what you write on your own time on a personal blog. This applies particularly if you are an at-will employee (true in most states in the United States).

If your blog is racist, discriminatory, or otherwise unacceptable to your employer and if that limitation has been spelled out in the company's blogging guidelines, you're toast. A few cases of employees being fired for blogging have been widely publicized. They include such employers as Delta Airlines, Google, British bookseller Waterstone and Wells Fargo as well as the U.S. Senate (see *dooced* in the Glossary). The companies in question are usually mum on exactly what happened.[15]

Two of the most high-profile incidents involved young staffers. Mark Jen was a new employee at Google who was fired after several weeks for griping in his blog about Google's compensation policies. He was swiftly rehired by Internet company Plaxo.com, where he immediately set about creating a set of public communication guidelines.[16] Perhaps the best-known case is that of Senate staffer Jessica Cutler, who was fired by her boss, Senator Mike DeWine (R–Ohio) after she blogged about her sexual escapades with members of his staff as well as a (married) Bush administration official. She promptly lost her job, posed for *Playboy* and signed a book deal. Hyperion published *The Washingtonienne*, Cutler's appropriately titled roman à clef, in June of 2005. (Lesson: life isn't always fair.)

Blogging guidelines published by large public corporations, usually technology companies, go to the other extreme, attorney Levin said, after reviewing a list of policies I submitted to her. Not only do they detail what an employee can and can't do, she said, "surprisingly, they offer advice for *how* to blog," IBM's Blogging Policy and Guidelines is a good example. Sample points:

- Respect your audience.

- Show proper consideration for others' privacy.

- Avoid topics that may be considered objectionable or inflammatory, such as politics and religion.

- Find out who else is blogging on the topic and cite them.

- Don't pick fights.

- Be the first to correct your own mistakes.

See the complete text of the IBM Blogging Policy and Guidelines in Bonus Resources. The difference between a policy and a code of ethics, or guidelines, is important when you're creating a blogging policy for your company. (1) A policy covers what you can and can't say for legal or company reasons. (2) A code of ethics talks about how to behave appropriately in the blogosphere. This should include tips on how to write a blog that invites conversation with your readers, etc. Together, a policy and guidelines should provide both directives and encouragement.

Michael Hyatt, avid blogger and CEO of Thomas Nelson Publishers, the largest Christian publishing house and a public company, employed a collective approach when crafting his company's blogging guidelines. He had a specific motivation for encouraging his employees to blog. He wants to make the mass-market publisher look more cutting edge and to attract a new kind of employee.

In March 2005 he wrote on his Working Smart blog, "Several of us [have] cooked up a list of Blogging Terms and Conditions. Our corporate counsel has also had a crack at it." He posted these under the title, "Corporate Blogging Rules" and asked for public feedback from other bloggers. Several dozen responded. The consensus: the "rules" were too dry, too much legalese, and why the title "Rules"? Very unbloglike.

About ten days later, after incorporating much of the feedback, he posted a new set. This time he called them "Corporate Blogging Guidelines, Draft #2." I've included them in Bonus Resources at the end of this book, and I think they're worth a skim. The challenge in crafting guidelines is to balance competing interests: to encourage your employees to blog, to advise them of legal risks and, at the same time, to be crystal clear about what your company's policy is.

In summary, from the company's point of view, the following are vital:

- Clarify what topics are on and off limits.

- Be clear about whether or not employees can blog on company time.

- Specify whether a disclaimer should be included ("The thoughts expressed here are my own . . ."). See Resources section for sample disclaimers.

From the employee's point of view, keep the following in mind:

- Be smart and use your common sense.

- If you wouldn't want to see a particular blog entry published in the newspaper, then don't post it.

- If you're trashing your employer or divulging confidential information and are worried your boss might fire you . . . keep worrying.

DEALING WITH LEGAL ISSUES

If you really want to get down and dirty, here's a laundry list of legal issues raised by employee blogging: defamation, user privacy, intellectual property infringement, trade libel, trade secrets, federal securities fraud, securities violations (i.e., improper financial disclosures), employment issues and discovery (i.e., meaning a company can be sanctioned for failure to produce archived blog content).[17] Almost all these issues, as we've pointed out, can be addressed in your blogging guidelines. There's no need to fret any more about the legal liability associated with blogging than you would over a leaked email, an indiscreet conversation with a member of the press or a clandestine meeting by one of your employees with your biggest competitor.

For pointers to learn more about blogging and legal issues, see Bonus Resources. And of course consult your own legal counsel.

THE MOTHER OF ALL FEARS: LOSING CONTROL

It can happen. With dizzying speed. If you've never been a part of the giant echo chamber that is the blogosphere and you're suddenly thrust into it, having the steering wheel snatched from your fingers can be painful. That's what happened to lock manufacturer Kryptonite in the fall of 2004. Someone posted an odd fact to a discussion forum—Kryptonite's U-shaped bike locks could be picked with a Bic pen. Bloggers quickly picked up the story. It spread like wildfire through the blogosphere, and then to MSM. Within days it was a top news story and even on network TV. Meanwhile, Kryptonite said nothing. They didn't respond to the bloggers; they didn't post anything about the problem on their Web site.

The story quickly became apocryphal in the blogosphere. Kryptonite was the poster child for "companies who don't get blogging." Their brand was forever tarnished. No one would ever trust Kryptonite again or purchase a new lock from them. Only trouble was, the story wasn't entirely accurate. It turns out that Kryptonite did NOT have its head in the sand. The company was not gnoring the brouhaha in the blogosphere. PR manager Donna Tocci knew exactly what was being said, she told me a year later, and in fact had been monitoring a number of blogs for months.[18] She was just too busy arranging the complicated logistics of an international lock exchange program to respond to the bloggers. (Kryptonite, owned by Ingersoll-Rand, didn't have exact figures on what the exchange cost. It was estimated to be $10 million. More than 380,000 locks worldwide were exchanged in ten months.)

Frankly, Donna said, she wouldn't replay the incident any differently. As she put it, "The bigger PR nightmare would have been to say we will exchange all your locks and then not be able to." She emphasized that Kryptonite spent an enormous amount of time *offline* attending to both the problem of the defective locks as well as the PR ramifications. And she is convinced that her customers (who are distributors and dealers—not consumers who walk into a bike shop) were not online, reading blogs. "The cycling industry is not very advanced as far as online," she said. "A lot of bicycling publications don't even have full Web sites." For at least a year following the episode, however, if you typed "kryptonite bike lock" into Google, the top results were blogging entries critical of the company. So, as far as her online identity, she had in fact lost control of her brand— at least for a period of time.

This is a messy story that doesn't have a clear ending. But this much you should take away from it. Keep your ears open to the buzz in the blogosphere. Have a contingency plan in place to respond if a crisis involving your company suddenly becomes the blogging topic du jour. If you don't have a corporate blog (and your employees aren't blogging on behalf of your company) then jump onto several influential blogs and leave a brief comment. This way, no matter, what remedies and steps you are taking offline, you'll get credit for being responsive.

Call this the ugly underbelly of the blogosphere, if you will, a place where rumors and innuendo and half-baked stories can spread around the world in hours or days. But even though the blogosphere can be a scary place, there are steps you can take to protect your company, educate your employees, and tackle your personal fears of blogging. These include creating blogging guidelines, learning how to write a blog, understanding how blogging technology works, and exploring the new metric of ROB (return on blog).

Of course, studying what other companies are doing with public-facing blogs may be the best way to combat your fears and learn how to use the speed and reach of blogging to your advantage. Which brings us to a baker's dozen of creative ways you can use blogs as a marketing strategy, as a communications tool and as a way to connect with your customers.

CHAPTER 4

A Baker's Dozen: 12 Plus 1 Ways to Use a Corporate Blog

"Eventually, most businesses will use blogs to communicate with customers, suppliers and employees, because it's two-way and more satisfying."
—Bill Gates, chairman of Microsoft, April 2005[1]

General Motors' global vice chairman Bob Lutz was itching to get back at reporters who were giving the financially troubled GM so much bad press. He didn't know much about blogging but he knew how to write in an engaging, direct style. So while flying back from a business trip to Europe in December 2004 he composed an open letter to GM's customers, telling them his thoughts about the aging Saturn line. He emailed it to Gary Grates, then his chief North American communications manager, with a query, "What do I do with this?"

Grates and his team had been charged with launching a blog for GM and he knew just what to do with it. Wheels tend to grind slowly in mega corporations. While a snazzy looking template had been designed for the blog, no entries had been written or inserted. GM's blog, at fastlane.gmblogs.com, wasn't public yet. It was still a shell waiting to be fed with fresh content.

So Grates moved quickly. He dropped Lutz's letter into the template. It was the first blog post, dated January 5, 2005.[2] Thus was GM's FastLane blog born. Here's what Lutz wrote:

After years of reading and reacting to the automotive press, I finally get to put the shoe on the other foot. In the age of the Internet, anybody can be a "journalist." This is the first of many commentaries I will make on this forum, and I'd like to begin with, surprise, some product talk—specifically, Saturn products . . .

What would you do if you had a brand whose customer service reputation was that high for that long despite having a narrow, aging product lineup? I, for one, would first get down on my knees and thank the Maker for the finest retail network in the industry. Then, I would set to work replenishing the product portfolio.

Since then, Lutz and a handful of GM's other senior executives have posted hundreds of entries to the blog. Close to 10,000 customers have responded with comments, rebuttals, criticism and ideas. Most of these have been published to the blog, typos, bad grammar and all. (The comments are reviewed quickly before being posted. Only those that are profane or racist or otherwise unacceptable are rejected, Grates told me.) The result is a mosaic of voices and a mountain of opinion about GM's cars.

What does this mean for GM? Lutz says the blog gives him—and by extension the number-three company on the Fortune 500 list—a direct line to customers, something he's never had before. "I just love getting the direct, unfiltered feedback. But I also love radiating my personal opinion," he said in an October 2005 podcast. The Fast-Lane blog enables the top brass at this multinational to hear their customers' voices firsthand. Customers in turn have a public forum to talk to GM's executives about car design, engine capacity, fuel efficiency and all the other fun stuff that auto geeks like to hash over. They complain; they praise. They also talk to one another.

Of course you might ask how relevant GM's blog is now that the company is in what many are calling a death spiral. With a loss of $10 billion in 2005, a shrinking market share, 30,000 layoffs, ballooning health care costs and the specter of bankruptcy, you might reasonably ask if blogging weren't just a wee bit of a diversion from more serious matters at hand. It's a valid issue: how to handle the bad times as well as the good on a corporate blog.

The short answer: be crystal clear about the focus of your blog. If you're only going to talk about products (whether they're cars or widgets), then say so in an easy-to-spot place on your blog layout. Oh, and say it again when something big or controversial about your company comes up in the news. But you still need to expect some push back, either from your regular readers or from other bloggers. Once you've opened a blogging channel, readers—and corporate blogging observers—are going to expect a level of transparency that you may not be prepared to offer.

GM's director of new media Michael Wiley explained the "no comment" policy of FastLane this way:

We have stated repeatedly that the FastLane Blog is about Cars and Trucks. I guess you could say that is our editorial niche. We are not a corporate issues blog. Our core readers want to read about our product and they do not like (it) when we deviate. A corporate issues blog is a whole different animal that brings with it heightened legal and regulatory concerns.[3]

1. THE BIG IDEA: BLOGS AS A MARKETING STRATEGY

Bad news or not, the point is that GM is using a blog as an instant publishing and marketing channel that bypasses mainstream media. Any organization can use a blog in this way. It's a way to put your own version of the story out there and to get feedback. And sure, you might be accused of a bit of spin. Or not being totally transparent. But at least you've opened a window into your company. It may not reveal your corporate soul but it's a view your customers haven't had before. If you write engagingly and candidly, they'll likely applaud you for it.

What else can you do with a blog? By now, business blogs are no longer a novelty. Corporate blogs are proliferating faster than you can say "ping" (which is what blogs say to each other or to the blog search engines) and companies are using them in a variety of ways. *External,* or public blogs, as we've seen, are generally used as a PR and marketing channel. *Internal* blogs (sometimes referred to as "dark blogs") are being used for project management and knowledge sharing.

The common thread—whether blogs are public or behind a firewall—is fast, low-cost communication. Blogs are searchable. Blogs are real-time. Blogs are easy to add information to, if you're the publisher, and easy to leave a comment on, if you're a reader. Combined with Web feeds (aka RSS) that alert subscribers with updates, they're an efficient channel with none of the drawbacks of email, clogged inboxes or spam.

With so many attractive features, you might well ask if blogs will *replace* other online channels. Blogging purists insist that blogs will change everything. For example: PR is dead! That meme rippled through the blogosphere in 2004 and 2005. The thinking was that press releases (often distributed online these days) are artificial, inauthentic and, most poisonous, boring. And many of them are. But you can use a blog to *complement* old-fashioned PR. And yes, sometimes, in lieu of press releases.

The reality is that, for the time being, blogs will not replace traditional marketing and communications strategies. Blogs will not supplant static Web sites (yet). Fortune 500s will still spend millions on TV and print advertising, although some of those millions are already moving online. In December 2005 MSNBC made history when they made the largest ever online ad buy: $1 million to promote three of their network TV programs on 800 blogs and several news Web sites.

What blogs do is complement existing channels. They offer you a new opportunity to create buzz, loyal customers, a stronger brand— and possibly, increase your revenues. And I mean *possibly.* Connecting blogs with the bottom line is still a bit tricky for most companies. Think of blogs as a powerful, cost-efficient tool to *add* to your marketing communications mix. And while they may seem a bit daring right now, an experiment, an extra you don't need to bother with, that's changing fast. Why? Static Web sites are just that. No fun. Not engaging. Often not effective. An interactive blog component built into a corporate site will soon become a standard part of up-to-date site design. Trust me. This is not a radical notion.

We started with the umbrella idea of blogs as a marketing strategy. Now let's narrow that down to look at more specific ways you can use a corporate blog—for thought leadership, community building, customer relations and online status alerts. For conferences and events, for advocacy, as an adjunct to PR, for branding and to spur e-commerce. Finally, we'll look at fan blogs (customer evangelists who market for you) and at something new—an all-blog viral marketing campaign. And the 13th in our baker's dozen: blogs as the new Web sites.

And, yes, by the time you read this there may be a dozen more categories of corporate blogs that didn't exist at press time.

2. THOUGHT LEADERSHIP

One of the most established ways to use a blog, especially for consultants and entrepreneurs, is to become a thought leader—an acknowledged expert—on a narrowly focused topic in your industry niche. The folks who write the best of these blogs are smart. They write well and they have something to say—they really are experts. Also key, they write consistently, if not every day, then several times a week.

Well-known author, speaker and entrepreneur Seth Godin writes one of the most popular "thought leadership" blogs, as they're called in the blogosphere.[4] Seth riffs on stuff he bumps into in real life and relates it to the marketing maxims he outlines in his books. ("Be remarkable." "Tell a story.") One example: he blogged about his experience, jet-lagged and unable to sleep, interacting with a hotel clerk in the middle of the night. Godin wanted to use the locked exercise room. The accommodating clerk agreed to flout the rules and open it up for him. The takeaway: the encounter spoke volumes about the hotel chain's attitude toward customers, far more than a platitude about "customer service" in a glossy brochure.

Most CEO or senior executive blogs fall into the thought leadership category. A handful you should check out for style, substance and/or smart writing are: Jupitermedia CEO Alan Meckler's blog; ReturnPath CEO Matt Blumberg's blog; Dallas Mavericks' owner Mark Cuban's blog; Go Daddy founder Bob Parsons's blog and Six-Apart cofounder and president Mena Trott's blog.[5]

3. COMMUNITY BUILDING

Technology companies typically use blogs to engage customers, who are often developers themselves, in an ongoing conversation about the features and functionality of their products. One example is blogging pioneer Macromedia, the software company now owned by Adobe. Macromedia launched a blogging strategy in 2002 (ancient history) when it asked five of its community managers to create their own blogs, distinct and separate from the company Web site. A community manager is a manager of a specific product line who is charged with building buzz and a "community" of users—whether prospects or customers—around the product.

"Giving the community managers a platform on which they can use their own voice, that was our idea," said Tom Hale, then the vice president in charge of developer relations.[6] The thinking was that customers (i.e., developers who use Macromedia's products) would find the community managers more credible than someone from corporate communications—particularly if their blogs were seen as *separate* from Macromedia.com.

In addition to responding promptly to questions about Cold-Fusion or Dreamweaver or Flash, each community manager could proactively post known issues about bugs—and have that information ripple immediately through the blogosphere. So successful was this approach that Macromedia now maintains an industrial-strength aggregator page for all its employee blogs as well as selected customer blogs.[7] RSS or Web feeds are available in 16 languages, including Farsi. This is corporate blogging on steroids. In addition to subscribing to selected blog feeds, you can sort and search every blog on the page in myriad ways—by date, most recent posts, most popular, language, etc.

This approach to blogs as a marketing strategy mimics the development of open source software. It's in keeping with the information-sharing ethos of the blogosphere. You release your code on the Web and encourage others to bang away at it. By letting everyone into your sandbox they get the bugs out and create new products *for you*.

Microsoft, with an estimated 2,000 or more active bloggers among its 50,000 or so employees, takes a similar approach. Some say that Microsoft's employee bloggers (again, many are technical experts) are not collaborating on product development with outsiders so much as engaging in community-building conversations.[8] The buzzword is evangelizing. By interacting with like-minded partners or customers, listening to their concerns, responding and being accessible, the employees are acting as company ambassadors.

Microsofties also monitor the blogosphere for mentions of Microsoft and Office product names. And then jump on to other blogs to leave comments correcting misimpressions or adding new information. Monitoring other blogs, as we'll see in chapter 9, is a key first step to incorporate blogs into your marketing and PR strategy.

4. CUSTOMER RELATIONS

Then there are upbeat company blogs that provide a blend of customer service and useful tidbits of information. This is an especially good use for a blog if your customers are online when they're using your service or software. Intuit has blogs for each version of its QuickBooks line. QuickBooks Online, Intuit's pioneer blog, was suggested by an employee and then championed and greenlighted by general manager Paul Rosenfeld. It offers up an informal blend of tips and news, written by a handful of Rosenfeld's team of 100 or so staffers. Rosenfeld says he doesn't really care what topics are covered on the blog. "The goal," he told me, "is to build confidence in prospects and customers by sharing relevant information in a transparent, open and honest way. To build confidence in our product."[9]

Keeping up the QuickBooks Online blog has proven to be a bigger challenge than Rosenfeld initially envisioned. It's one thing to empower your employees to blog, which he has done, as an especially collegial and open-minded boss. It's another to prompt them to do it on a regular basis. In mid-2005 Rosenfeld tapped one of his product managers to act as an "online" community manager. Her job is to oversee the blog (i.e., to encourage contributions from other staff) as well as to respond to questions posted to the QuickBooks Online discussion board.

Paul still occasionally posts. He's got the bloggy voice down pat and doesn't worry about the occasional spelling error. He titled a post in late 2005, "Did we cause you inadvertent pain?" and wrote:

Great Expectations.

Did you have these when you signed up for our service? Did they come true? Didn't they? We want to know, so drop me a line by responding to this blog. Specifically, our Marketing Team works very hard to see to it that prospective customers understand what QuickBooks Online Edition can do and what it can't. Sometimes, however, we don't go far enough.

Typical of an effective blog entry, Paul's is a bit tongue in cheek, makes a literary reference (Charles Dickens) and yet asks a heartfelt question: Are you getting what you want out of the online edition of QuickBooks? He really wants to know.

5. STATUS ALERTS

Another increasingly common use for blogs is to provide customers with a real-time "status" page for a Web-based service. These status blogs don't always make for great reading. They tend to be written by the tech team and feature phrases like "due to a temporary service degradation, you may not be able to access your XYZ service." They're a fine use for a blog unless you're truly in the midst of a crisis. If that's the case, customers want to hear something from your top executive that's written in plain English and transparently explains what the "temporary" problem is.

Blog software company SixApart experienced several crises in late 2005 when TypePad, its popular blog hosting service, went down and was unavailable—or ran excruciatingly slowly because of an overload on the servers. The company made several missteps by not providing enough information to its online customers (myself among them) during the outage. Irate customers didn't want a dry "status alert." They wanted an apology and an explanation from the CEO. And they wanted it in real-time. In other words, on the company blog. (They got it eventually in a long blog entry from CEO Barak Berkowitz outlining the technical challenges of moving millions of blogs to a new server.)

Blogs are tailor-made for any kind of Web-based product or service. Just be sure you meet your customers' expectations for instant updates—even if you're in the midst of a crisis and your attention is focused on solving the problem, not communicating with your customers.

6. CONFERENCES AND EVENTS

Virtually every conference related to technology and the Web has a blog counterpart these days. And many events that don't have an online focus also use a companion blog as a marketing strategy. The blog fires up the buzz ahead of time, before the event begins. During the sessions the blog chronicles the atmosphere surrounding the conference: the back conversations in the hallways, digital photos of attendees, colorful details about the venue. Downloads of the speakers' PowerPoint presentations or other handouts are often made available through the blog.

You might think this would dissuade people from attending. To the contrary, a conference blog creates a record of the high points of the sessions (useful to read even if you attend) and functions as a permanent, searchable resource to market your next event. That's assuming you leave the blog up even if you're not adding new entries to it. You'll get more mileage out of blog marketing if you let your blog stay live; it will still appear in Google search results.

Another approach is to create a short-term blog that "expires" after a certain date. (This is also a good way to venture into public blogging. "It's a time-limited blog," you can tell your boss.) *Fortune* hired a marketing agency to do just that for *Fortune*'s 2005 Innovation Forum (November 30–December 1, 2005). The conference blog launched at the URL businessinnovation2005.com as a way to drive registrations for the event. In addition to contributions to the blog from conference speakers, a freelance blogger/journalist was hired to post entries. After the event, the URL of the blog was changed to theinnovationinsider.com and the prominent graphics and links to the forum were removed. The blog now covers the general topic of innovation.

7. ADVOCACY

Not surprisingly, non-profits—some with small marketing budgets and many with big goals—have embraced blogging. The March of Dimes, which focuses on preventing birth defects, created a group blog site offering free blogging tools to families of preemies. The writers can share their experiences—often emotional and difficult—

with a one-time story or in an ongoing blog. Similarly the American Cancer Society created a bloglike community site, Fabulous at Fifty, to collect individual stories and promote colon cancer awareness.[10]

Planned Parenthood is using blogs in several ways. The organization has a blog-like feature on its home page at plannedparenthood. org with the latest entry prominently displayed, followed by a "read more" link. It's really a device to feature in-depth essays on the many issues that Planned Parenthood addresses, from abortion and adoption to sexual health and sexuality to religion and politics. Dig a little deeper and you'll find another blog, Truth Be Told, as it's called, written by Karen Pearl, interim president of the Planned Parenthood Federation of America. This one is more personal.

The more politicized advocacy world is also venturing into blogs. Amnesty International had launched four blogs by the end of 2005, each targeted at a key issue: human rights violations, the death penalty, denouncing torture and violence against women.[11] "They're trying to cultivate a blogger army," Internet strategist Cheryl Contee told me, by reaching out to younger, tech-savvy audiences. But initially the blogs were nothing more than a publishing platform for relevant news items. The entries weren't signed and expressed no "voice" or opinion on the part of Amnesty staffers. "The blogs are in a proto stage where people recognize them as important," Cheryl said. "But they're taking small steps. They're risk-averse."[12]

Much bloggier is NARAL's (National Association for the Repeal of Abortion Laws) Bush v. Choice blog at bushvchoice.com. It's written by "Jessica" (no last name). Jessica, we learn through a link at the top of the blog, is a twenty-one-year-old feminist with a master's degree in Women's and Gender Studies from Rutgers University. She writes with an edgy informal voice and offers opinionated commentary on legislative happenings around the country. Another blog that offers up a good mix of opinion and news is the National School Board Association's BoardBuzz blog at boardbuzz.nsba.org.

Which of these approaches is more effective? Generally, the edgier or bloggier blogs I've described above have more impact.

Blogs that are used primarily as publishing vehicles for news or essays are really just a content management system that organizes information by date or topic. There's nothing wrong with that if it suits your needs and goals.

8. ADJUNCT TO PR

Search giant Google uses its official blog as a complement to press releases and for issues management, David Krane, Google's vice president of corporate communications, told me. The blog is managed—and written or edited—by the corporate communications department. Can you hear the sirens of the blogging police? Yes, this approach violates one of the best practices you may have heard about blogging: don't let your PR people write the blog. Well, guess what. It's a brave new bloggy world out there. You can use a blog any way you want as long as it's useful and engaging for your readers. Google's Krane thinks of the blog as another channel that operates side-by-side with traditional corporate communications. He explained: "You can be more flexible with the language. You can be more informal. You can integrate visuals in an elegant way. In addition, the blog is a great opportunity to get everything off our chest and get it out to the world the way we want to. We may use the blog in conjunction with press releases or in lieu of. We can be proactive or reactive with the blog."[13]

In other words, if the *New York Times* or the *Wall Street Journal* doesn't get a news story quite right (from Google's point of view), the company can immediately clarify the issue in the blog—or at least add their own spin. During the protracted dispute over Google Print (the company's controversial initiative to scan every book in print and then make full or partial text available through search) several Google staffers, including CEO Eric Schmidt, defended the project. Schmidt posted a quick note to the blog the same day that an op-ed piece with his byline ran in the *New York Times*. His entry included the full text of his newspaper column. In effect Google was ensuring even wider distribution of Schmidt's column, in addition to archiving it permanently on the blog. (Presumably, Google obtained reprint permission form the *New York Times*!)

Most important, Google's blog often linked to articles critical of the company's stance on copyright. Not the kind of thing you would include in the straightforward language of a press release, right? By acknowledging naysayers, Google managed to make itself look more credible.

Think about that for a minute. It's fundamental to what makes corporate blogging an effective PR channel. Of course, you might ask whether the rules are different for this new corporate behemoth. In November 2005 Google's market value was $112 billion, making it bigger than Coca-Cola, Inc., Time Warner and Cisco Systems, Inc. If anything, when it comes to blogging Google is held to a higher standard of conduct. If Google can use blogs as a complementary PR channel—and get away with it—then why can't you?

Another way to use a corporate blog as a PR tool is to offer the informal—or some might say, backstory—version of an official announcement. Readers love this kind of thing. I call it the *People* magazine approach to PR. Blogs are the perfect petri dish. When Internet pioneer Vint Cerf joined Google in 2005 as Chief Internet Evangelist, the company issued a press release listing his credentials as one of the architects of Internet standards and protocols. (He's also a Presidential Medal of Freedom winner.) The same day, Vint posted to the Google blog:

Cerf's up at Google!

9/08/2005 08:21:00 AM

Posted by Vint Cerf

<u>The news is out</u> that I will join Google on October 3 as Chief Internet Evangelist (I tried for Archduke, but it didn't work). What I really like about Eric, Larry, Sergey and the whole Google family is its collective and eminent practicality and seemingly boundless creativity. In fact, my recent interactions

with many of Google's senior staff have simply underscored my admiration for the extraordinary talent at Google that has been assembled in a short amount of time. Google has come so far since the early days!

The phrase "the news is out" links to the press release in the news section of Google's site. You may be asking if Vint wrote this entry himself. My bet is that he did, with a little editorial polish from corporate communications staffer Karen Wickre. When I wrote this, she was spending one-quarter of her time as editorial director of the blog. She organized a loose editorial calendar, was on the committee that approves entries submitted for the blog and did light-touch editing on all the entries submitted for the blog. Yes, you heard me right. Google has an editorial committee for its blog. And so can you. In fact, you can designate a chief blogging officer as Stonyfield Farm has done.

9. BRANDING

Stonyfield Farm, the world's largest producer of organic yogurt, employs a blog editor who oversees two blogs prominently featured on the company's Web site. The purpose of the blogs is to extend the company's mission of promoting healthy kids and a healthier environment. Blog editor Chris Halvorson was hired in March 2004 after Stonyfield's CEO, Gary Hirshberg, decided blogs were the next new thing to add to his progressive company's site. A fan of Howard Dean's presidential primary blog, Gary was out ahead of his employees on this one. Chris told me that she wasn't familiar with blogging when she applied for the job.[14] So she quickly brushed up before the interview. She was hired shortly afterward and launched the company's blogs in April 2004. To her amazement, Stonyfield attracted national attention as a pioneering corporate blogger. She was profiled in a *Wall Street Journal* article and has been asked to speak all over the country. Is this branding via blogging? You bet.

Another creative blogger, J. D. Iles, is the energetic proprietor of a small New Hampshire–based sign-painting shop. He blogs daily at SignsNeverSleep (usually at 3 AM, soon after he gets up) as a way to visually record the signs he's producing as well as offer gentle patter about the weather, and what's new in his shop. His goal is for prospective customers, no matter where they're located, to find his blog, to peruse all the signs he's painted and ultimately to place an order. To become, in other words, what blogger and marketing consultant Hugh Macleod calls a "global microbrand." (See box.)

Most appealing to J.D. is that "I'm a believer at hacking away at big proposals with a teaspoon a day. A blog is something you can hack away at for 10 minutes a day and at the end of four months you have something phenomenal."[15]

What's a Global Microbrand?

by Hugh Macleod

It's a small, tiny brand that "sells" all over the world.

With the Internet, of course, a global microbrand is easier to create than ever before. But they've existed for a while. Imagine a well-known author or painter, selling his work all over the world. Or a small whisky distillery in Scotland. Or a small cheese maker in rural France, whose produce is exported to Paris, London, Tokyo etc. . . .

And with the advent of blogs this is no longer just limited to people who make products. . . . Any service professional with a bit of talent and something to say can spread their message far and wide beyond their immediate client base and local market, without needing a high-profile name or the goodwill of the mainstream media. . . .

Once I created my own fledgling global microbrand (i.e. via this blog) I started helping other people do the same. A bespoke Savile Row tailor. A Master Jeweler. A small vineyard in South Africa. It was professionally the most compelling idea I had ever come across. I was hooked.

Of course, "The Global Microbrand" is not conceptual rocket science. . . . What excites me about it is the fact that I now live in a small cottage in the English boonies, and career-wise I'm getting a lot more done than when I lived in a large apartment in New York or London, for a fifth of the overhead. For one-fiftieth of the stress level.

It seems to me a lot of people of my generation are locked into this high-priced corporate, urban treadmill. Sure, they get paid a lot, but their overheads are also off the scale. You know what? It's not sustainable.

However, the Global Microbrand is sustainable. With it you are not beholden to one boss, one company, one customer, one local economy or even one industry. Your brand develops relationships in enough different places that your permanent address becomes almost irrelevant.

There are thousands of reasons why people write blogs. But it seems to me the biggest reason that drives the bloggers I read the most is this: we're all looking for our own personal global microbrand. That is the prize. That is the ticket off the treadmill. And I don't think it's a bad one to aim for.
(Adapted with permission.)[16]

10. E-COMMERCE

According to online market research firm comScore Networks, blog readers are 30 percent more likely to buy products or services online. And shoppers who visit blogs spend 6 percent more than the average customer.[17]

Still, a blog as accompaniment to an e-commerce site may sound like a poor match. If the blog content says buy, buy, buy, it's not bloglike. If the writing is clumsily and overtly promotional, it's a bore. But online fashion retailer BlueFly.com came up with a twist: a blog titled Flypaper: Stuck on Style at flypaper.bluefly.com. A typical entry:

The Pope Wears Prada

Who would have known that under Pope Benedict XVI's sacred robes lurked a pair of red Prada shoes? From the Independent (U.K.).

Related Links: To match the holy crimson robes, may we suggest his Holiness wear this red Prada sarong or carry his things in this clear Prada tote?

This was posted by Wendy at 10:05 AM on November 4, 2005, one of three snappy entries she made that day. Of course, the underlined words link directly to Prada items in BlueFly's trendy online store. The editorial formula is simple but wickedly clever: a sentence or two riffing on a fashion or celebrity news item. Followed by Related Links (a play on this oft-used feature of online writing) that point to specific items for purchase. Even if you're not a fashionista, this makes for awfully good reading—and more to the point, inspires a click-through to the suggested Prada accessories for the Pope.

Wendy is one of a team of that BlueFly hired to write the blog. Which is a key point. Creating and sustaining this kind of blog requires editorial talent you may need to hire.

Another good example of a blog as adjunct to an e-commerce site is one of my favorite resources, 800-CEO-Read.com. Blogging in this case is a natural adjunct to selling books. The blog entries are engagingly written reviews of recommended business books, with a link to the purchase page where you can order online.

11. CUSTOMER EVANGELISTS

What do Vespa motorscooters and Starbucks have in common? They're strong brands that breed passionate customers. Customer evangelists are so engaged, in fact, that they blog about DVD rentals, Palm Treos, motorscooters and Starbucks coffee *for free* just for the thrill of being associated with the brand. Fan blogs are an intriguing subcategory of corporate blogs. Often they pop up without any prompting from the company. A few of the best-known customer evangelist blogs are Mike Kaltschnee's hackingnetflix.com, Jim Romenesko's starbucksgossip.typepad.com and Andrew Carton's blog.treonauts.com. The bloggers "feel like they own the brand, that it's theirs," said Jackie Huba, author of *Creating Customer Evangelists*.[18]

Vespa, on the other hand, worked with a PR agency to set up its two fan blogs at vespausa.com/VespaBlogs. The bloggers are not paid but they do get compensated with loaner scooters. Independent fan bloggers often make a bundle of money by selling affiliated products through their blog sites. Companies can choose to: (1) ignore their fan blogs, (2) try to shut them down or (3) capitalize on them as free marketing by officially endorsing or otherwise cooperating with the blogger. You choose the right answer.

12. VIRAL MARKETING

The newest new thing may be a blog-based marketing campaign. Budget Rent A Car created the category in 2005 when it commissioned consultant B. L. Ochman "to do something viral to make their image a little hipper and cooler," she told me.[19] Her response was to orchestrate UpYourBudget.com, a 16-city, four-week treasure hunt with cash prizes totaling $160,000. The contest, aimed at 20-somethings, was conducted solely via tips and videos posted to the very cool multimedia UpYourBudget blog. (Contestants were given clues to find an actual sticker in a public place in one of the cities throughout the U.S. Drawings were held once a week for four weeks.) The blog-based contest generated lots of buzz via ads placed on other blogs as well as other bloggers talking about it. No press releases, no press conferences, no other publicity.

.   And the result? Several thousand people registered on the blog to play the game. The blog itself received over a million unique visitors in four weeks. Budget's total outlay for the campaign was approximately $350,000, BL said (including the $160,000 in prize money and $23,000 spent on blog ads). A fraction of the millions that parent company Cendant spends each year on advertising.

13. BLOGS AS THE NEW WEB SITES

Finally, and most prosaically, blogs are the new corporate Web site. In late 2005, the trend of relaunching a corporate site as a blog was just emerging. There are lots of reasons to do this, including improved search engine rankings, a simple content management system that enables non-technical employees to instantly update your site and the ability of a blog format to more effectively transmit the knowledge inside your company to your customers. Matt Blumberg relaunched ReturnPath.net, his email company, as a blog in the fall of 2005. (The new URL is returnpath.biz.) When I spoke with him in October they were just shaking out the kinks. "What's going to be challenging is that it's going to require us to think like a publisher," he told me. "Our main objective is to disseminate the intellectual capital inside our company to our customers."[20] Six executives were contributing to the blog, one of them acting as managing editor. "Welcome to Return Path's Online Resource for Email Marketers" runs across the top of the new home page. The blog prompts visitors to subscribe to the RSS feed for update alerts on new white papers, webinars, industry news, tips and strategies. And also offers an email sign-up box.

CHAPTER 5

Should the CEO Blog?

"In ten years, most of us will communicate directly with customers, employees, and the broader business community through blogs. For executives, having a blog is not going to be a matter of choice, any more than email is today."
—Jonathan Schwartz,
president and COO of Sun Microsystems[1]

As more companies embrace the idea of blogging as a powerful way to listen, learn and talk back to customers online, the question of whether the CEO—or COO, VP or other top executive—should blog has become a popular one. The short answer is yes. And if you believe high-profile blogger Jonathan Schwartz's claim above, you better get cracking so you can master this new way of communicating before your competitors do.

On the other hand, should Oprah blog? Probably not. What about Bill Gates? Umm, no. If you're too much in the public eye and also happen to be CEO of a public company, it's likely your every word will be parsed for hidden meaning. You'll find it hard to let loose and be truly authentic. Your customers, competitors, the press, analysts, investors—not to mention your employees—will be searching your blog for inside information and clues to the *real story* about your company's financial condition or future direction.

By the way, I'm using the word CEO as shorthand for top executive. If you're a solopreneur or captain of a microenterprise (remember J. D. Iles of SignsNeverSleep in chapter 4?), then you're your own CEO. This chapter is for you. If you're the head of a multibillion-dollar Fortune 500 company, or a multimillion-dollar private company, this chapter is for you, too.

A small number of public figures aside, that leaves millions of top dogs who might in fact make good bloggers. And if you're looking for first-mover advantage as a CEO blogger, you've got it. Only 7 percent of the 131 CEOs polled in PRWeek/Burson-Marsteller's 2005 CEO Survey[2] said they are currently blogging. Many are skeptical about starting their own blog. Another 18 percent plan to start a corporate blog within the next two years. Don't adopt a wait-and-see attitude when it comes to starting a blog, however. It doesn't make sense. One of the most important ideas I want you to take away from this book is the following: blogging is not all that hard to master. It's more an approach and a way of thinking than a tool or a technology. You don't need a nine-month project plan to launch a blog.

Boeing Vice President Randy Baseler's blog, "Randy's Journal," launched in 48 hours after Boeing Web designer Chris Brownrigg got what he called "the blogging phone call." Baseler had decided on the spur of the moment that he wanted to start a blog in January 2005 on the eve of the unveiling of archrival Airbus's new super-jumbo, the A380.

Though Chris knew nothing about blogs when he was tapped by the higher-ups, he dove into the project by looking at dozens of other blogs. He chose Movable Type, popular blogging software licensed by many companies, installed it on a test server and quickly created a prototype. "(Management) resisted calling it a blog," Chris told the packed audience at the Blog Business Summit, eager for the inside story of Boeing's blog. He got around that by titling the Web page: "Boeing Blog: Randy's Journal." An important detail because he wanted the blog to come up on a Google search for "boeing" and "blog."[3]

Author, entrepreneur and blogger Seth Godin sets a high bar for CEO blogging. He wrote in a much-quoted post on his own blog, "Blogs work when they are based on: Candor, Urgency, Timeliness,

Pithiness and Controversy (maybe Utility if you want six). Does this sound like a CEO to you?" He continued: "Short and sweet, folks: If you can't be at least four of the five things listed above, please don't bother . . . Save the fluff for the annual report."[4] In other words, according to Seth, CEOs aren't cut out for blogging. OK, it's true that blogging isn't right for every CEO, particularly if they tend to be cautious and conservative by nature. But it can be done if your CEO has the right temperament and the right touch, likes to write, has something to say and values honest communication. So there is no short answer to the question "Should your CEO blog?" The long answer is more complicated, but I'll begin by saying, "It depends."

Are You Nuts?

I know, I know. The idea of taking on (or suggesting that your boss take on) yet one more responsibility, one that you have to pay attention to regularly and that involves writing (which many people hate) may seem insane, but consider this. A 2005 study commissioned by the *Wall Street Journal* and the Business Roundtable revealed that 39 out of the 44 companies responding said their CEOs have an open email policy with employees and *personally respond* to every single email they receive from staffers.[5] According to the *Wall Street Journal*, such a policy "is a powerful leadership tool that can nip crises in the bud, boost morale, uncover new ideas, and cut through corporate red tape. In the post-Enron era of CEO accountability, reading employee email helps the boss appear hands-on and accessible."[6] Sun Microsystems' cofounder and CEO Scott McNealy told the *Journal* he gets 150 emails a day from employees who tell him what competitors are up to. He replies to each one, although often with a one-word "thanks." Pfizer CEO Henry McKinnell Jr. said he gets 75 internal emails a day. He answers them from his BlackBerry and considers them "an avenue of communication I don't otherwise have."

So really, the idea of penning a blog—even if it's an internal blog for employee consumption only—isn't so far-fetched. CEOs (maybe you're one of them) are already doing a lot of writing. Why not do it more efficiently? Instead of a one-to-one message, why not a communication from one-to-many thousands?

A blog could replace those late-night sessions tapping away on a BlackBerry to respond to hundreds of emails. Yeah, I know what you—or your communications director—is thinking. "But all I have to do is shoot him or her a quick 'Thanks' and my employee is satisfied with our little exchange. Won't blogging take a lot more time and involve a lot more thought if I have to write out whole sentences and paragraphs and pages? How will *that* save me time?"

Valid question, but it's a matter of weighing pros against cons. Starting an internal blog can be a lot more efficient in the long run and also enable you to better communicate your point of view, your decision-making process and your ideas.

Pros:

- Reach more employees with a single message.

- Appear (and in fact be) more accessible.

- Create a searchable archive of your thoughts.

- Employees' questions and feedback will be permanently recorded on the blog.

Cons:

- Master a new style of communicating.

- Create an expectation that you'll be posting regularly to the blog.

- Put yourself out there—your writing ability and your thought process—for everyone to scrutinize.

- The writing (a pro for those who love to write) can be difficult.

INTERNAL CEO BLOGS: THE NEW MUST-HAVE EXECUTIVE TOOL

The first thing to note about an internal CEO blog is that it's a knowledge management tool. Think of it that way, and not as a private diary of your innermost thoughts, and you'll be a lot more comfortable. It works like this: You post a new entry on a regular schedule. Strive for once a week. If you need a break because of travel or an extra busy schedule, post a short message on the blog saying when you'll be "back." (See tips on how to *write* a blog in chapter 7.)

If you're launching the blog as a way to shift from answering hundreds of individual emails, your communications folks need to do some internal training:

1. Encourage employees to subscribe to the RSS or Web feed for your blog so they're alerted every time you post a new entry.

2. Encourage them to leave comments on the blog instead of emailing you.

In addition, you should publish clear guidelines as to what topics are off limits or inappropriate, whether for legal reasons or just "to play nice." Be clear about what your employees can expect to hear from you, and what you'd like to hear back in return.

One of the few internal blogs by a Fortune 500 CEO that has been widely publicized is that of Intel's Paul Otellini. He launched his internal blog in December 2004 with the following entry:

While this is intended as an internal blog, I recognize that it will become public—welcome to the Internet! As a result, please recognize that I may be a bit limited in my comments and responses to protect Intel, and that we may exercise some editorial privilege on your comments for the same reason. I want to be clear on this up front. This is the price of entry to this blog.

The following language was included as a reminder to employees: "Paul's Blog is a private communication for Intel internal use only. Please do not forward or distribute outside the company." But several weeks later someone copied the contents of the blog, pasted them into a Word document and shipped them off to a reporter at the *San Jose Mercury News*. (The excerpts are now publicly available as a downloadable PDF.)[7]

Was this a crisis? Not really. Intel got high marks for having an executive blogger. (Paul was COO when he started the blog. He became CEO of Intel in May 2005.)

An internal blog can create a rich company history. Say a new employee comes on board and wants to get up to speed on the water cooler gossip of the past six months. This is where the knowledge management function of a blog comes in. You can search previous entries by month, by topic or category, by keyword, etc. Over time, the blog becomes a permanent, archived record of your ideas and opinions, your take on industry events and company happenings. Unlike those thousands of employee emails that you receive— and reply to—and that fall into server oblivion after they've been deleted.

Still not convinced? Feeling too much pressure to be brilliant? It doesn't matter if individual blog entries knock the socks off your readers with their profundity or eloquence. They don't have to. It's the accretion of writing over time that creates a knowledge base, a record of *who you are* and *how you think* that is valuable and creates a lasting impression.

Common Objections

Two of the most common questions I hear from potential CEO bloggers are:

- What about stuff I'd like to write about that I only want certain groups to read?

- I'm busy; why can't I just get someone in PR or corporate communications to ghostwrite the blog for me?

You can start a password-protected blog open only to you and selected senior officers and/or their assistants, to track meetings and minutes or big ideas and directives. In addition, the newer generation of enterprise blogging platforms (see chapter 8 on blogging tools and technology) has permission levels and restricted access built into them. You decide who can read what. If someone is not an authorized reader, he or she won't "see" your blog entries.

Interestingly, this multiple-view, restricted-access is already built into popular personal blogging platforms like LiveJournal. Mena Trott is cofounder and president of SixApart, which acquired LiveJournal. She told me, "Blogging is a life recording mechanism. What we'll see in the future is that we'll be recording even more moments of our lives. Instead of being afraid of saying too much because it's online, we'll have the confidence that only certain audiences can see certain things."[8]

Another use for an internal blog: encourage your sales people to share stories about wins and losses on a group blog. Blogger and writer Halley Suitt calls this "just-in-time inventory of ideas."[9] In other words, use a blog to slash the communications lag in your company to almost zero. Halley's example: a sales blogger posts a pertinent anecdote at 9 AM about why she couldn't close a sale with a high-end customer. You read this information (it describes a lack in your product's feature set) just in time to take the anecdote to your product development meeting at 11 AM.

The other common question that execs ask when faced with penning a blog relates back to time: Why can't someone else write it for me? A legitimate question, but I'll counter by asking why your executive assistant doesn't answer those hundreds of emails from employees? Don't you trust him or her to decide what's important, what's not, how to respond, etc. No? Kind of defeats the purpose, doesn't it? Ghostwriting won't work for a CEO or executive blog. Readers will sniff it out. As Sun's Jonathan Schwartz puts it, "Most important, write the blog yourself. Authenticity is paramount. Some senior executives hire people to write their blogs. Don't bother. It's like hiring someone to write your email."[10]

Executive ghost blogging is going on at lots of companies.[11] But so are bad press release writing and speeches brimming with platitudes. Doesn't mean it's right just because it's happening. Here's a real-life anecdote about ghost blogging as emailed to me by a British journalist. He asked that he and the European company in question remain anonymous.

> An executive starts a blog. He flies a lot and has lots of time to compose his thoughts. The blog starts to get lots of traffic. Other executives get curious; they're jealous. So another executive starts one up, but he can't write well enough (English isn't his native language) and doesn't have the time. He asks his assistant to blog for him. Then the communications people get involved and they turn to an outside PR company. Turns out the PR folks have their own team of ghostbloggers on hand for occasions like this. They take up the mantle. Now the exec just sends occasional thoughts for inclusion in the blog.

Does this make a mockery of executive blogging? You decide. My perspective is that this is another *kind* of blogging. It's a publishing platform for an executive rather than an authentic communications channel. So maybe it's not a fraud, but it's not really a blog in the sense that we're talking about either.

But there is a way to get off the hook when it comes to the time demands of blogging. You don't have to write your executive blog all by yourself. And I don't mean delegate to an editor or ghostwriter; I mean collaborate. Group or team blogs are becoming increasingly common. As long as each person signs his or her blog entry, the collective blog will retain authenticity. It will come across as a chorus of individual voices speaking to the same topic or theme.

Which can be equally engaging. Group blogs will be ubiquitous by the time you read this. They're a great way to create ongoing content and to keep up momentum. Take a look at Hill & Knowlton's Collective Conversations blog at blogs.hillandknowlton.com.

You can probably think of lots of creative things you could do with a group blog. Invite a guest expert blogger from outside your company to contribute. Appoint an articulate employee to blog for a week and spar with you on a hot topic.

The Skinny (Sort of) on Intel CEO Paul Otellini's Internal Blog

If you're wondering whether all this effort is worth it, listen to Paul Otellini's second entry on his blog:

> First of all, let me say that I was blown away by the response to the Blog. We received over 350 comments in the first 24 hours, with more coming in every day. I did not read them all, but read many of them. I would like to do two things in today's update. First, I want to expand on the platform topic in response to some of the posted comments . . .

He was referring to Intel's shift to Web-based, or platform, applications in contrast to memory chips or microprocessors. This is a big deal, both in terms of Intel's product focus and for the company's branding and advertising strategy which rests on "Intel inside." His employees responded with comments like these:

> Like the Blog, especially the "straight talk" style. My feedback is, keep it up, tell us the positive stuff, but tell us the negative too—in the same straight manner, don't sugar coat it. Much of the comm we get from Sr. Mgt. these days has too much "happy" spin on it. This is a refreshing change. As always, tell us honestly what you need us to do—we'll get it done.

And another:

> The Blog was a good idea. Whatever Paul's intent with this
> device, it gives the implication of personal interaction and a
> level of empathy and discourse. One of Intel's biggest prob-
> lems today in its sprawling hugeness is a lack of shared focus
> and a sense of isolated kingdoms with little top down commu-
> nication. The Blog does "top down" one step better, it's almost
> like a subordinate brown bag luncheon with the top dog.
> Kudos.

That kind of feedback is surely manna to the ears of an ivory-
towered executive. Since the leak, Paul's blog has been under wraps,
but I spoke with Intel spokesman Tom Beermann in September 2005
to get an update.[12] He told me that Paul posts a new entry every
week to ten days so employees can "hear the voice of the CEO" on issues pertinent to Intel and the tech industry.

As for which employees are interacting with the blog, Beermann
said it's a wide range, from "manufacturing to marketing" but generally "not senior managers." He feels the blog can reach into the
trenches in a way that an internal newsletter or other publication
can't. Beermann insisted that Paul "enjoys the interaction and plans
to continue." But there are no plans to make the blog public. Nor
have there been any further copy-paste "leaks," as far as Beermann
knows.

Here's the kicker. In September 2005, I met two senior-level Intel
executives at a private party on the West Coast. One, in marketing,
told me she regularly reads Paul's blog and often makes reference to
it in her team meetings when she's trying to inspire everyone with a
bit of top-down vision from the CEO. The other executive, in merg-
ers and acquisitions, flatly said he never reads the blog and could
care less what "Paul has to say about [Hurricane] Katrina." So there
you have it. A sample size of two. Covering the spectrum of what I
suspect are common reactions from more than 100,000 Intel em-

ployees to their CEO's blog. "It's great" versus "who cares." But the point is, they all have an opinion. And they know he's blogging.

ADVICE FROM TRAILBLAZING CEO BLOGGERS

So on to the big question. If blogs are time-intensive, if they require thought and effort to write, and if their ROI is rather soft (although satisfying if your blog gets lots of comments and feedback), what makes them worth the risk of sticking your neck out in the blogosphere? The answer: their value and utility as a communications vehicle. Communicating is the real job of most CEOs, isn't it? Communicating a message, clarifying it, repeating it. Whether the audience is internal or external.

The desire to communicate more easily and more broadly and to connect with more stakeholders is the prime motivator for most senior executive blogs. Wrote Boeing's VP of Marketing Randy Baseler in his first blog post in January, 2005:

> Welcome to my new Web journal . . .
>
> I hope it will help solve one of my biggest frustrations—not being able to talk with everyone as often as I like about what's going on in our industry and our company. Either I'm in a different time zone, or in a meeting or at another commitment, so this Web space can be a place where you can go to find out my thoughts and opinions.[13]

Sun's Jonathan Schwartz had similar words when he started his blog in June, 2004:

> OK, I'm starting a blog. Why shouldn't an officer of a public company start a blog? Hey, life is short . . .
>
> What's a blog? It's basically an on-line journal—a whitespace—into which I can offer perspectives, opinions, and insights, and I can link to others and their views, etc. Others

can link to me and send me feedback, creating a massively connected community and open dialog. Reality TV comes to corporate America.

Why am I doing this, starting a blog?

. . . To change the format and fidelity with which what I say is transcribed. No more comments from the pundits "in context." Now you get them straight from me.

(Also) to get unfiltered feedback from the community. If you want to reach me, I'm "jonathan.i.schwartz at sun.com". I promise to read it all, but please don't count on responses (I'm a bit deluged already).[14]

And to immediately squelch the idea that he would reveal insider information about Sun's business, he added:

You'll see thoughts on the future (but absolutely no forward looking statements—for all insight into our business performance, please refer to our regularly scheduled filings at the SEC). Thoughts on my favorite Web services. Even good reading. Maybe good eating. This is an evolving medium, time will tell.

I promise to listen—from all the constituencies we serve (customers, stockholders, developers, consumers, suppliers . . . all).

Hello, world.

In an unpublished interview[15] with *BusinessWeek*, Jupitermedia CEO and blogger Alan Meckler talked about why he started his blog:

It looked like an interesting sort of way for the CEO to get the message out. I felt I could turn the blog into Internet media commentary. It (has) evolved . . . I now write more frequently. I write nearly every day, from 50 to 300 or 400 words. It's therapeutic, and beneficial for the company . . . I call it the way I see it, within reason. I write about what I think is happening on the Net. I try to weave in as often as I can how we're doing as a company, using it as a promotional tool. I'm not trying to hide the fact.

Meckler happens to be the largest stockholder in Jupitermedia so he doesn't have to answer to his legal department. He often writes about Jupiter's many acquisitions with disarming frankness, giving the backstory behind a deal and including a link to the official press release. Still, he doesn't cross the line. "I'm not giving away inside information," he told *BusinessWeek*'s Stephen Baker. "I don't write (the blog) to pump the stock."

Similarly, GM's Bob Lutz explained why he blogs: "If you get the feedback through your corporate organization it's going to be somewhat filtered. People won't give me negative emails."[16] And he seems to enjoy correcting the media whenever he can, as he noted in his first blog post on FastLane (see chapter 4).

Thomas Nelson Publishers' CEO Michael Hyatt has another motivation for blogging: making his company look more progressive. "I'm trying to change our culture from closed and opaque to open and transparent," he told me. "We're using it as a recruiting tool."[17]

Another CEO publisher, Berkshire Publishing Group's Karen Christensen, also uses her blog to let some light into the publishing process. "Publishers typically have something of a castle drawbridge mentality. They send out information in polished, finished form, then pull the bridge up. The whole open-access movement is putting them under pressure to be more collaborative, and blogging is our chance to show our approach."[18]

So we've covered the time factor and the communications advantage. What about the "voice" of a CEO blog? Also, what *don't* CEOs blog about and how do they get into the groove of blogging regularly?

EXTERNAL CEO BLOGS: THE PERFECT BULLY PULPIT?

The ingredients of success for a public-facing CEO blog are similar to what's required when talking internally to the troops. Just as an internal blog builds up a critical mass of insights over time, so does an external blog develop more gravitas the longer you keep at it. Ideally, the blog attaches a voice to the company through the words and style of the executive writing it. A legitimate question to ask, however, is this: Is a CEO blog "the" voice of the company? What about employee blogs? Perhaps it's better to say that a CEO blog can *help* tell the story of the company. The story you want customers and the media to listen to.

It's a subtle difference, but it touches on one of the most oft touted reasons for a large corporation to blog—giving the company a human voice. Flamboyant Dallas Mavericks basketball team owner Mark Cuban insists that his blog should be the *only* mouthpiece for his company. "A confused message is worse than no message," he told me.[19] He doesn't allow any of his employees to blog on behalf of the Mavericks.

What's Off Limits: The Balancing Act of a Senior Exec Blog

Though they are equally strapped for time, small or private company CEOs may feel freer to express themselves. They aren't beholden to stockholders or to analysts or bound by SEC regulations about financial disclosures. And they do express themselves freely, blogging on topics that often range far afield from their company focus. Go Daddy founder Bob Parsons, for example, relishes being controversial. In June 2005 he segued, in a long blog entry, from reliving the horror of 9/11 to endorsing abusive interrogation at Guantanamo Bay. The response was a blogstorm of criticism for his "right-wing" political views, along with some positive comments as well.

Parsons listened. He backed down slightly from his position, after learning more about interrogation techniques, and blogged a semi-apologetic follow up. In it was a mixed message:

> I also have been accused of mixing business with politics because I put a link to my blog on the Go Daddy home page. I will say that the opinions here are mine personally. This is, after all, my personal blog. Go Daddy, the company, has no political leanings of any kind.

A CEO with a personal blog that has no connection to his company? Um, it doesn't normally work that way. That's the definition of corporate or business blogging, after all. The blog is representing the business in some way.

I interviewed Bob by phone not long after the incident. He was ebullient about blogging, insisting again that his blog at bobparsons.com was separate from his domain name registration service at godaddy.com. (Despite the fact that there is an obvious link to Bob's blog at the top of the Go Daddy home page.) He told me his blog "has nothing to do with [Go Daddy]. But there are benefits that impart to the business and there are consequences to the business."[20] Splitting hairs maybe. In any event, there's no doubt that the brouhaha surrounding Bob's politicized statements drew more attention to his blog, already highly-trafficked with 10,000 visits a day. Customers were not defecting from Go Daddy, Bob said, despite his candor on the blog. In fact, new registrations were up in the following months.

On the other hand, public company CEOs or senior officers like Boeing's Baseler or GM's Lutz often hold themselves in check on their blogs when it comes to commenting on negative company news. This drives blogging observers wild. What about transparency? Openness? Telling it like it is. Not going to happen, say their spokesmen. If the focus of the blog is product—airplanes or cars—that is all the exec is going to talk about.

When former Boeing CEO Harry Stonecipher stepped down in

early 2005 after it was revealed that he had had an affair with a subordinate, Randy Baseler was mum about the incident. Finally he wrote:

> We've had an interesting couple of weeks as a company, that's for sure. But none of that has made a bit of difference down here on the ground. The focus at Commercial Airplanes is, as always, on our customers and on the future.

"Interesting" doesn't quite work as a descriptor for scandal, does it? Equally deafening was the silence on GM's FastLane blog after the announcement in March 2005 that GM was forecasting an 80 percent earnings drop for 2005. Several weeks later, Lutz referred lightly to "reallocating resources (human and financial) to pull some other programs ahead and get other vehicles to market sooner." Presumably those "human resources" were GM's much publicized layoffs of more than 30,000 workers.

Neither of these circumlocutory approaches to the "real news" is truly satisfying. But there isn't an easy answer to this kind of situation, is there? Most likely, big corporations are not going to drop all pretense of spinning their message—even if they have a blog.

BOTTOM LINE: THE VALUE OF WRITING

If you accept the notion that the ability to write clearly and cogently reflects the ability to think clearly, then writing is a crucial skill for an executive.

Matt Blumberg, ReturnPath CEO, agrees. Writing is a lost art for top executives, he says. "When you get in business you stop writing. You do emails and PPTs." His blog at onlyonce.blogs.com gives him a space to work out his ideas. He told me:

> To do a good job (as a CEO) you have to be very articulate. You have to be able to think clearly and write clearly. Writing helps

me clarify my thinking about things. And writing in the blog particularly does because it's so short. I don't have time to write a 10-page white paper but I can refine my message down to two paragraphs for a blog posting. It really helps me cut to the chase.[21]

Zane Safrit, CEO of Conference Calls Unlimited, started blogging to refine the business strategy for his small but growing teleconferencing company.[22] The initial impetus was to differentiate his company's services in a crowded commodity market. "I'd been racking my brain to find another way to market," he told me. He'd tried direct mail (expensive and a bust); he'd invested tens of thousands of dollars a month in pay-per-click advertising on Google and Yahoo (not effective in bringing CCU new customers).

Then it hit him. Blogging was the perfect way for him to embody his central marketing message: you get a real person—a human voice—when you call CCU. Only problem, Zane said, was that he didn't consider himself a "word craftsman."

....

"My blog is a place for me to occasionally climb up on a podium and pound on my bible and work out ideas by writing."
                                                    —Henry Copeland, founder and
                                                            CEO, Blogads.com

....

No matter. He dug in and started writing his blog. By the time I spoke with him, just over a year after he'd started blogging in earnest, Zane was posting several times a week about current events, the economy, outsourcing, health insurance and other stuff that interests him. More to the point, the quality of his writing had improved noticeably. It was clearer, crisper, more cogent.

Zane said he writes "for an hour or two" every day. Ninety percent of the time he's online when he is blogging, typing directly into TypePad's interface. He "publishes" almost immediately. Then goes back later to do a quick edit, if needed. He starts out with a goal of "four lines." But often finds he writes 1000 words. "With a cup of coffee the sky's the limit," he says.

Blogging as the Ultimate Icebreaker

It's too soon to tell exactly where the phenomenon of CEO blogging will go. I hope it will become an accepted way of communicating in corporate America. Will it replace email, as Jonathan Schwartz predicted in his words at the beginning of this chapter? Not yet. For now blogging remains an executive status symbol of sorts, but it's not just a badge of coolness. A blog gives customers, potential partners, even media a handle on what your values are, how you think and what your key issues are—*before* you walk into a meeting or an interview. A blog may be the ultimate icebreaker for a senior executive.

CHAPTER 6

The New ROI Is ROB (Return on Blog)

"We're not worrying about the ROI.
We just assume it's there."
—Christine Halvorson,
Chief Blogger, Stonyfield Farm

So what's the bottom line on corporate blogging? Ouch. I knew you'd ask. Can you put aside the dollars and cents thing for a minute? I know that online marketers are mad for metrics. Page views and unique visitors; clicks and conversion to sale. Blogs, a kind of Web site, do fit into the online category where those metrics normally apply.

But blogging is a different beast and I want you to consider some non-traditional measures of value. It makes sense, doesn't it? This brand-new communications tool calls for a brand-new measuring stick to evaluate its effectiveness. Like buzz or word-of-mouth marketing or the feedback from your customers. Because, really, bottom-line ROI is out when it comes to corporate blogging. What's in is possibly more valuable, even if it can't be precisely—or at least quantitatively—measured.

What's in is ROB (return on blog). It's all about connections, conversations, discovery, information, word-of-mouse, leverage, amplification and efficiencies. Oh, and blogging is still something of a fashion statement for a Fortune 1000 company, which almost guarantees you media attention. If you move fast, you'll reap first mover advantage. This won't last long but it's a positive result for now.

Buzz, for the unindoctrinated, is that halo of positive conversation around your brand. It's created by what your customers and others are saying about your company. There's even a term for it: "buzz marketing." (And a book, *Buzzmarketing* by Mark Hughes.) When it's blogging buzz, it means you're a company that's willing to take risks, to try something different and to open a direct line of communication with your customers. It means you're willing to take a little heat. Yes, even let your customers criticize you.

Next, think amplification and snowballing. If you post something provocative, newsworthy or oddball enough on your blog, it can get picked up and spread around the blogosphere within hours or days. New iPod owner George Masters was so thrilled with his new green iPod that, in his spare time, he created a 60-second video featuring flying iPods and colorful psychedelics set to 1980s pop music. He posted it to his site. A few blogs picked up the link to his homemade video and within weeks it had been downloaded 64,000 times.[1] What would that kind of viral marketing cost if you tried to engineer it? Millions? Total cost to Apple in this case, *zero.* Apple didn't have to do anything to make this passalong marketing happen. A customer evangelist created the ad for them and other bloggers were intrigued by it. Blogging is that fast and that powerful.

MEASURING THE CONVERSATION

That explains the viral aspect of blogging. But what about the conversations? If the blogosophere is a collection of conversations, how do you put a value on that? It may not be a hard metric but there *is* an equation: multiple one-to-one conversations equals community building.

I asked Christopher Barger, IBM's Blogger-in-Chief, how he was measuring the ROI of IBM's blogging efforts. "Blogging is a medium whose currency is the sharing and exchange of expertise," he told me. "We believe we have more than 300,000 experts working for

IBM. This is a medium that's almost custom-made for us." His point is that IBM's business is technology so it's only natural for IBMers to "join the conversations being carried on by blogging communities around the world. We see this as an unprecedented opportunity."[2]

At the same time, IBM is not foolish enough to think that blogging will solve any of its core business problems. As Jim Finn, IBM VP of communications, told me, despite the publicity surrounding the launch of IBM's blogging initiative in May 2005, blogging " has nothing to do with reducing layoffs and increasing revenues . . . It's another channel for communication; it doesn't cure cancer."

Still, six months after the blogging initiative was announced, the number of active blogs on IBM's Blog Central was up 70 percent, to nearly 2,300 blogs, Barger said. Over 5,000 employees had registered a blog, although fewer than half were actively blogging. This is a typical ratio, by the way. Lots of folks, whether at home or at work, express interest in blogs and then don't stick with it.

Barger continued:

Just as blogging requires companies to re-think the way they communicate with their audiences—adjusting to no longer being in complete control of the message or conversation, no longer just broadcasting a message out via one-way channels and hoping they sink in, and so on—blogs also require us to re-think how we measure the value of the investment of our time and resources.

Blogs aren't about selling things—that's neither the purpose nor the promise of the medium. So I can't tell you that, thanks to blogs, IBM has sold 10,000 more widgets than last year— that's not how it works. The value of social networks isn't measured in dollars. The ROI comes in the form of the individual relationships and affinities built through the communities you join and the conversations you have. The value is in the knowledge you share, in the lessons you learn, and in the viewpoints you help to influence through blogging.

It all sounds rather grand and fuzzy. But IBM isn't the only one talking this way about the ROI of blogging. Scott Anderson, director of Enterprise Brand Communications for Hewlett-Packard, is in charge of their enterprise or business-to-business blog program as a way to foster conversations between HP and its B2B customers. He uses terms like "conversational benchmarking" and "community involvement." He told a conference audience in December 2005 that blogging was indeed effective for HP and that top executives like Rich Marcello, senior vice president and general manager of Business Critical Servers, were proof positive.[3] Marcello was just wrapping up his first year of blogging. He wrote in a blog entry dated December 5, 2005:

> Well, I've been writing this blog now for about a year. The other day I was thinking about what I was trying to accomplish when I started last December and whether or not I actually did what I set out to do. I think I have. In a nutshell, I wanted to show you a little bit more about who I am as a person and what I really believe on many different topics. No hype, just a really direct and honest conversation on a host of topics. Hopefully, you've felt some of that in the writing and sometimes, at least, found some of the topics helpful. For me personally, it's been really useful to write down as honestly and crisply as possible what I believe.[4]

Despite being a senior-level executive, Marcello looks to be a gentle soul, judging from the photo on his blog, and from his writings. If you buy into the concept that blogging puts a human face on a large corporation, then Marcello's is one example. If you want some harder data, however, there *is* a way to compute it. Though you have to dot a few lines to make a direct connection between blogging and business results.

SHOW ME THE NUMBERS

Here are some examples of how you can make the connection between blogging and hard numbers.

- Microsoft's chief blogger Robert Scoble does in fact have a day job. He operates the handheld video for Channel 9, Microsoft's community site for developers at channel9.msdn.com. It features deliberately amateurish-looking video interviews, along with a discussion board, wiki and other geeky tools. The site, which launched in April 2004, has never gotten a penny for advertising. "It's just word of mouth," Robert told me. "No PR. No links from Microsoft.com." Yet Channel 9 had "2.8 million unique visitors" in October 2005, he said. All a result of buzz that rippled through the blogopshere. It started no doubt on Robert's blog, where every so often he casually mentions Channel 9 and some neat new video they've made. And got picked up from there.[5]

- ACCABuzz, the informational blog started in 2004 by the Air Conditioning Contractors of America (the largest U.S. trade association for heating, ventilation, air conditioning and refrigeration contractors), draws 15,000 visitors a month. Many find their way to the blog through Google searches, ACCA's VP Business Operations and Membership Kevin Holland explained to me. "Our blog posts rank very high in Google for certain searches that our main site (despite its relatively high page rank) would never have showed up for," he said. As for ROI, he reported, online sales of technical manuals and software have more than doubled and new memberships are up 50 percent. All because of the blog? "No, but it sure played a role," he said.[6]

- Finally, J. D. Iles, owner of the sign painting business in Lincoln, New Hampshire (I talked about his blog in chapter 4), told me he can attribute 10 percent of his total sales in 2005 to his SignsNeverSleep.com blog. That's $35,000 out of $350,000 for this microenterprise. How does he know? Well, he runs a small shop and he asks every customer where they first heard about him. J. D. says that he is convinced that the blog gives "a small business like mine the reach and marketing power of a Ford without spending millions and taking 50 years to do it."[7] His blog features an appealing mix of photos (extremely useful as a way to showcase his work, he says), inside glimpses of how he runs his shop and occasional personal commentary.

If You're Dead Set on Making Money from Your Company Blog

Sell T-shirts. Honest. This is the new, cool thing to do on a blog. T-shirts, caps, mugs—they're all part of blog schwag. Sure, you can run those little Google ads (Google AdSense) down the side of your blog. Click-throughs may garner you some commission dollars. But it's much cooler to sell stuff with your blog name on it. You can set up a store through Cafepress.com or Spreadshirt.com in minutes.

BoingBoing.net sells T-shirts. Americablog.com sells T-shirts (random sampling: "George Bush is a Category 5 idiot.") Of course, the more off-color and controversial you can be with your schwag, the more you'll sell.

This means naming your blog isn't an idle task. Try and come up with something short and catchy that wears well on a T-shirt. Although your company name will work fine too. Don't get so clever that your blog isn't immediately recognizable as connected to your company.[8]

USING STANDARD WEB METRICS

You can apply standard Web metrics to corporate blogs but with some caveats. Blogs are Web pages. And it's no more difficult to measure traffic to a specific blog entry, defined by its unique URL, than it is to measure the number of visitors to a page on your site. General Motors' FastLane blog had 250,000 visitors a month, or 8,500 visitors a day, in mid-2005. But it's more complicated than that.

GM's director of New Media, Michael Wiley, told me he spent "five hours a night" for the first four or five months after GM's Fast-Lane blog launched, "trying to track reaction to the blog."[9] He used Google to see if the blog was showing up in Google searches on GM brand names. And Technorati, to determine what ranking the blog had, given the number of in-bound links from other blogs. Ultimately, he was frustrated. The measurement tools aren't mature enough yet, he said. When other blogs—as well as articles in mainstream media—quoted from GM's FastLane, he didn't have a way to measure it, other than anecdotally.

The "amplification" of blogging is what is difficult to capture, he said. It's like playing the telephone game. By the time you've reached the end of a chain of quoting and requoting from a blog—or simply referring to the name of the blog or the company—you've created plenty of buzz. But it's not something you can easily attach a number to. Although a new breed of online market research firms is trying hard to do this. Companies like Intelliseek and Cymfony specialize in text-mining and text-analysis of blogs in order to provide their customers with metrics—number of mentions as well as trends and patterns of discussion—relating to the blogosphere.

You can also count the number of comments left by readers. But don't get too hung up on this. Some blogs get dozens or hundreds of comments. Others get almost none. Stonyfield Farm's Chris Halvorson doesn't worry about the number of comments left on the company blogs. Normally it's only a handful. "It doesn't mean your blog isn't being read," she told me. More important to her is that the yogurt makers' quirky blogs create an impression on visitors to Stonyfield's cleverly branded Web site. There's lots of "moo" language on the site: "moos" releases and "all the moos that's fit to print." CEO Gary Hirshberg is the CE-Yo. "Maybe there's a little ping when you're in the grocery store," she said. You're looking at the yogurt display and you recognize the name so you reach for one of Stonyfield's products. Stonyfield's customers are organically minded so they tend "to vote with their pocketbook," she added. The blogs are neatly tied into the company's brand image—small, family-centric, friendly. In fact, Stonyfield is the largest organic yogurt producer in the world and the third most popular U.S. brand.

The Secret Sauce for Any Corporate Blog

by Steve Rubel, MicroPersuasion.com

Corporations interested in blogging need to add value to people's lives. That's the biggest key to a successful corporate blog that keeps people coming back.

So what do I mean by add value? I mean give us a reason to read your blog. Give us something we can't find anywhere else. Provide information that your customers, partners and prospects care about, not necessarily what you care about. Be a resource and a connector."[11]

Measuring Your ROB

Yes, there is an ROB (return on blog) that is measurable. Even if you can't tie it to your bottom line. The obvious metric of success for corporate blogs is search engine results, as we've discussed. Another is WOMM (word-of-mouth marketing). This is a popular new marketing metric that's getting more and more attention.

As Pete Blackshaw, chief marketing officer of market research firm Nielsen BuzzMetrics put it: "Blogging is putting WOMM on steroids. They're giving greater currency and permanence to word of mouth. WOMM up till now has been dismissed as fleeting, ephemeral, non-quantifiable . . . but now with blogs our thoughts, feelings, opinions are getting codified. Blogs are proof positive that there really is a digital trail to word of mouth."[12] And it can be positive or negative. Blackshaw studied the thousands of comments left on GM's FastLane blog and determined that 45 percent of them were negative. But that didn't make the blog any less effective.

WHAT PROBLEM DOES BLOGGING SOLVE?

The human desire—and business need—to connect. In real-time. As Microsoft's überblogger Robert Scoble puts it: "What's the ROI of speaking in front of a conference audience? My audience (his blog readers) is thousands every day. Yet I see executives regularly take the time to fly around the world to speak to audiences of hundreds."

I asked Scoble, what if you have just a handful of readers? He shot back in an email. "If you know Bill Gates and Steve Jobs read you every morning, wouldn't that be a trip?" And in fact, he's pretty sure that his boss, Gates, does read his blog.[13]

Asking questions, as Scoble does, rather than making solid pronouncements, is a good way to think about the value of blogging. The late and revered management guru Peter Drucker might have been able to help us qualify blogging this way; he was a master of the Socratic approach. His 1954 classic *The Practice of Management* posed three fundamental questions:

- What is our business?

- Who is our customer?

- What does he consider value?

Look at blogging from the vantage point of those three questions and it may help you answer the ROI question. In other words, if you understand what business you're in, who your ideal customer is, and what he or she considers useful or valuable, you'll know if your blog is on target or at least, in the middle of the right pond, and if it is telling a story that ripples out to the right people.

Measuring Buzz

Intelliseek/Edelman white paper

In the pre-blog world, "buzz" was created by news, stunts and events—both online and offline—that captured consumers' imagination and got talked about, written about and spread around. Buzz was measured and gauged by news clipping services, online click-throughs and hits, noticeable increases in brand sales. In much of the pre-blog world, advertisers and public relations professionals had vast amounts of control over the tone, timing, content and release of information and announcements.

Today, however, "news" and new ideas surface immediately from any variety of online sources, including blogs, some of them totally unexpected and off the radar. Often, news emerges in rich-media formats that include audio links, still images and video links. Bloggers can appear overnight, gaining traction and a reputation in a matter of days or weeks rather than building it over years.[14]

The Ultimate Measure of Success: A Happy Blogger

Ultimately, the satisfaction of the person writing the blog, whether it's a CEO or a small businessperson, is what determines the success—and staying power—of a blog. In an AOL survey of 600 bloggers[15] nearly 50 percent reported that blogging was a form of "therapy" and was their prime motivator. Pat Cleary, the prolific blogger for the National Association of Manufacturers, where he is senior VP of Communications, fits the profile. He blogs every night from 9 PM to midnight, after his day job, to produce a steady stream of newsy, opinionated riffs on legislative issues impacting NAM. "You first and foremost have to have a passion for writing, even if you don't consider yourself a writer," he told me. "I don't think it's ability as much as passion."[16]

CHAPTER 7

Top Ten Tips to Write an Effective Business Blog

"Dance like nobody's watching . . ."[1]

The quotation above is from a popular country western song, but it applies to good blogging. Write from the heart. Take a few risks. Be passionate. Be honest. Know what you're talking about but don't be afraid to ask your readers for help or feedback. That's what makes a blog good reading. It doesn't matter whether you're a solo consultant establishing yourself as the go-to expert or a Fortune 500 company that wants to communicate directly with thousands of customers. You must adhere to basic blogging etiquette if you want your blog to be a blog.

The informal style of writing, the first-person voice, the point of view, the topics you cover—the stuff you choose *not* to mention; often a concern on a corporate blog—are all part of the slightly messy ball of wax that is effective blogging. Messiness is key. I don't mean that your writing should contain typos or sloppy grammar. I mean that you have to let go of corporate-speak and polished prose, if that's what you think of as business communication.

The essence of blogging is being real. And real isn't perfect. If you're the sole author of or a contributing writer for your company's blog, write as if it's an email to a knowledgeable friend or colleague. You can still be professional, but let your personality seep in. If you're managing the blog, give your blog writer time to develop a bloggy rhythm and writing voice. Either way, gauge the reaction from readers or other bloggers. If you've hit a nerve, blog some more on the topic and keep the conversation going. If a blog entry falls flat, move on to something else.

Really, to blog is to write the rough draft of your company story. Your press releases may be polished and vetted. Your blog should not be. Or at least should not *appear* to be. If you absolutely must have a blog editor or a senior manager approve entries before they're posted, then go ahead. Google does this with its official blog, as we learned in chapter 4. But your blog will be more effective and more engaging if you let your bloggers bypass legal and corporate communications—and just do it, within whatever guidelines you've set, of course.

As I mentioned earlier, using a blog as part of your communications strategy means creating a new form of marketing collateral. Of course, this editorial product is a demanding beast, always hungry for new content. If you're not a media company—and used to the steady drumbeat of deadlines—this can be a particular challenge. Thus, this chapter is a guide to effective blog writing and maintenance for those companies who are not primarily in the publishing business.

Here is my clip-and-save list of Top Ten Tips to write an effective business blog. In the rest of the chapter I'll tackle some bigger picture issues relating to creating blogging content as well as touch on each of the tips. I've also included pointers from other bloggers, ones that I find especially thought-provoking. Like a blog itself, this chapter is a collection of bits and pieces of useful information. It adds up to a resource that you can come back to, and troll for inspiration. I wish I could tell you that there was a ten-step plan to become a better blogger. Unfortunately, there isn't. Basically, you just have to wade in and do it. And keep at it. As my favorite journalism professor was fond of saying, "It's not quality . . . it's quantity." In other words, keep writing. Eventually you'll improve.

THE TOP TEN TIPS FOR WRITING A SUCCESSFUL CORPORATE BLOG

1. Choose the right topic (be sure it's specific).

2. Find your voice.

3. Invite a conversation.

4. Package what you write (ten Tips, five Rules, seven Ways).

5. Always, always link.

6. Write for Web readers.

7. Write for Google searchers.

8. Publish consistently.

9. Take risks.

10. Have fun (the "dancing" part).

If you're already blogging, you may find the tips above obvious, but they'll provide a useful refresher if you want to reinvigorate your approach to writing a blog. Whether you're a beginner or have been blogging a while, tips #2 and #3 are a real challenge—to find your blogging voice and to invite a conversation while at the same time establishing yourself as an authority. That adds up to the three Cs of blogging: be conversational, cogent and compelling. Good blogging is good writing. And good writing is hard.

"Blogs can make for a more open organization that engages at a deeper level with the customer. However, blogging can require an honesty and frankness that many organizations are not used to. Blogging also requires quality time from quality people with quality ideas—and it demands commitment week-in, week-out."
—Web content expert
Gerry McGovern[2]

CHOOSING THE RIGHT TOPIC AND
MAKING IT SPECIFIC ENOUGH

The best-read blogs are narrow in focus and often about hot-button issues. Take the MilkIsMilk blog penned by Alex Avery of the Center for Global Food Issues (a project of the conservative Hudson Institute). This is an advocacy issues blog focused on one specific project—dispelling the notion that ordinary, non-organic milk is not healthy. The blog has controversy written all over it. If you're an organic food nut you may find the blog infuriating. If you're a dairy distributor who relies on production techniques that include antibiotics or high-tech interventions, you'll probably love it.

It's a good example of a topic that works and has ongoing appeal. The issue is singular and complex; it's controversial and it lends itself to being picked apart over time. Key is that Alex himself is passionate and highly knowledgeable about the issues surrounding the use of technology in agriculture.

Let me repeat that. You've got to be passionate about the topic of your blog. Whether you're writing it yourself or managing a team of bloggers, it's got to inspire you. Or you'll quickly run out of steam and lose interest in your new publishing venture. Also worth repeating: a topic that's highly specific works best. If it's mortgages, write about interest-only loans. Don't write about the general topic of mortgages and refinancing. You'll get more attention from other bloggers interested in your narrowly focused subject that way—as well as higher rankings in search results on keywords that describe your topic.

Your blog has to inspire your readers. I asked author Rebecca Blood to ponder what's behind a blog that works. She responded: "Audiences magically collect when people begin writing about the things that matter to them most. Not a large audience—the right audience. The group of people who share a passion for the things you care about, however few or many they may be."[3]

On the other hand . . .

Like almost everything associated with blogging, it's OK to try a topic just because you think it might work or it fits the theme of your marketing strategy or ties in with your mission. Stonyfield's Christine Halvorson did just that when she initially launched five public blogs for her employer in the spring of 2004. One of Stonyfield's original blogs, The Daily Scoop, was an inside look at how things are done at the company, both in the manufacturing plant and in the front office. (I'm sure someone was in love with the catchy title.) But she quickly saw there was only so much she could write on the topic of yogurt. The Daily Scoop was discontinued.

Chris continued to publish four blogs on topics related to the company's environmentally conscious mission. Then she dropped two more. Now there are just two: one on babies and parenting (the YoBaby product line is Stonyfield's biggest seller) and one about life on an organic farm (written by a local farmer).

When I interviewed her in October 2005 she admitted that the "Baby Babble" blog was limping a bit. She was tapping a group of employees with young children up to the age of 24 months to write it, but their enthusiasm was waning. Her solution? Bring in an expert. Stonyfield had recruited renowned pediatrician Dr. Bill Sears to do some consulting for the company. Dr. Bill, as he's called, is the creator of the term "attachment parenting" and author of 30 books. Chris asked if he would contribute to the blog as part of his consulting duties. Sure, he said. He has agreed to answer a few selected questions submitted by readers. It's a perfect solution, Chris told me. His commitment is minor, but it makes a big splash on the blog, where his photo and bio are featured.[4]

John Nardini, executive vice president of marketing for Denali Flavors, had a similar experience when it came to choosing blog topics. He started four blogs in 2004 as a way of marketing the company and its unique niche. Denali Flavors is an $80 million company that supplies a line of 30 flavors as well as ingredients to the dairy industry. Two of the blogs ran out of steam. And his guess about which ones would succeed was dead wrong.

He predicted the character blog (featuring a moose, the company's mascot) and the company blog (about ice cream flavors and the dairy industry) would be most appealing. They were shut down at the end of 2005. Instead, Denali's blog about supporting a bicycling team to raise money for a Latvian orphanage (Team Moose Tracks) and his completely unrelated blog about personal investing (FreeMoneyFinance.com) have stuck.[5] Free Money Finance, in fact, has garnered attention from *Business Week* as a Top Ten Personal Finance Site and was also mentioned in a *Wall Street Journal* article.

And the connection of FMF with Denali Flavors' products? None. In fact, Nardini writes FMF anonymously. Nardini describes himself on the blog—disarmingly—as "not qualified to give advice on the topic (of money management). I'm not professionally trained in financial management. I'm a layman in this field." But he notes that he's a serious student of prudent investment and staying out of debt and has done very well by managing his own finances for the past 20 years. Personal finance is a hot topic and the blog draws a lot of traffic. It's "sponsored" by Denali's signature ice cream flavor, Moose Tracks, so that visitors who click on the quirkily drawn illustration of the moose are taken to the company's home page. Traffic to the main site is up 25 percent, Nardini said. Thus he's managed by a circuitous route through the blogosphere to attract widespread publicity for Denali.

This is a perfect example of a private passion, on an unrelated topic, driving a corporate blog. Your blog doesn't necessarily need to be "about" your products. In fact, unless you're making really interesting widgets, it's better if it's not. As Stonyfield's Chris Halvorson puts it, "If you're making paper clips and you're only in the paper clip business to make money, then you don't need a blog. But we're a company that produces yogurt with the intent of changing the world."

The takeaway: there's a flip side to choosing a topic you're knowledgeable and truly enthusiastic about. Your audience. If you're not connecting, if there's no interest, you'll soon find out. You need the energy and involvement of your readers to sustain your blog. You'll know whether your blog is hitting the mark by the comments your readers leave. Or if you haven't activated comments, by the traffic to your blog, by your rankings in Technorati, by email messages to the editor. (Important: there should always be an obvious way to contact you.)

Does Your Company Blog Need to be Controversial?

By Kevin Holland, VP, Air Conditioning Contractors of America

Organizational blogs and personal blogs are two different animals.

It's long been an accepted truth that a good way to build traffic to a personal blog is, in fact, to pick a fight with someone. Let's not forget that politics created the blogosphere as we know it, not business. Controversy sells. Get a good back-and-forth between a few bloggers with spittle flying between posts, and eyeballs will follow the conversation.

But an organizational blog exists for a reason other than drawing traffic. It exists to support the organization, to sell a product, to engage a constituency, to meet a mission. Picking fights for the sake of drawing eyeballs for their own sake doesn't do any of those things.[6]

FINDING YOUR VOICE

This is trickier than it sounds. Heck, you know the sound of your own voice, don't you? But when it comes to writing, it's hard to get the blend of personal and professional—of opinion and passion mixed with facts and research—just right. The best advice I can give you is to write your blog as if you're writing an email. I consulted with a Top 50 law firm in Washington, D.C., that wanted to incorporate blogs into their marketing strategy. One of their young lawyers was already blogging and they brought him into the meeting to learn more about how to do it right. I cringed when I read his blog postings. "Dry" doesn't describe how stiff they were. They were duller than press releases and loaded with long tortuous sentences, although they described impressive cases he was working on. I thought for a moment about how I might tactfully critique his writing style.

If you were writing your mother, I asked, how would you say it? He was taken aback. Perhaps, I prompted, something more on the lines of, "Dear Mom, Great news about the big case I've been working on . . ."

CC: WORLD

So if an informal writing style is foreign to you, you might start by applying the "Dear Mom" test. Or approach blogging as prolific blogger Doc Searls does. "Your blog," he says, "is your email to everyone." It's a perfect way to explain what prompts the writing of a blog entry as well as how you write it. The best blog writing is done in a personal voice. Much as you'd write an email to a close colleague. You have something to say; you want or need to say it right now. You write it off the cuff. You give it a quick read-over. You hit Send. It's a fast and easy way to communicate both important information and amusing anecdotes.

I asked Doc to elaborate on his "email to everyone" concept. He emailed back promptly:

> People often ask me, "How do you find time to blog?" And "Why do you write so much on your blog?" I usually reply, "How do you find time to email?" and "How many words do you email a day?"
>
> Since the beginning, most of my blogging material comes to me from email. Some of it is blog fodder, by intent. But a lot of it is just personal "check this out" correspondence. Often

I'll reply to the world rather than just to the sender. That's why I think of blogging as "cc:world". When you think of it that way, you realize it doesn't need to be nearly as complicated or time consuming as it seems.

P.S. I'm also often amazed at the "prolific" line. I can name many bloggers . . . who spend far more time and energy—and words—blogging than I do. But somehow the impression comes across (that I'm prolific). I think that's because my blogging style isn't much different than correspondence. It's like letter writing.[7]

By the same token, you're apt to eagerly read an email from a friend or close relative because you expect there will be an interesting or funny nugget in it. You're expecting a whiff of the writer's personality to come through in the message. Perhaps you nod in agreement or shake your head in exasperation when you read it.

The point is that reading an email—particularly a candid one—is an engaging experience. It's not like reading the bland corporate-speak that populates too many home pages of corporate Web sites. This is key. A blog really isn't a blog unless it's written in a certain style. It should reek of authenticity.

On the other hand . . .

Not to waffle but I need to point this out. If you choose to, you can use your blog as an instant publishing channel. You might insert news updates, snippets from Congressional testimony or headlines from the *Wall Street Journal*. And never offer your opinion or commentary. Never, in other words, insert an individual voice. Just be aware that if you do that, your blog is not really a blog. It's a publication in a blog format.

....

"Ask people to help you think. Most of the people who comment on my blog are helping me think. In other words, don't say, 'Blah blah blah. I'm an authority. Now talk amongst

yourselves while I go pat myself on the back.' Say, 'Gee, I'm not
that smart, but here's something interesting I'm noodling on. I've
gotten this far on these pieces. Help me out here . . . someone?' "
—*Joi Ito*[8]

YOUR WRITING STYLE: BE SIMPLE, CLEAR, CONVERSATIONAL

In other words, write well. Investor (and world's second-richest man)
Warren Buffett penned a preface to *A Plain English Handbook* published by the SEC almost ten years ago as a helpful guide to companies filing disclosure documents. He wrote:

> One unoriginal but useful tip: Write with a specific person in
> mind. When writing Berkshire Hathaway's annual report, I
> pretend that I'm talking to my sisters. I have no trouble pic-
> turing them: Though highly intelligent, they are not experts
> in accounting or finance. They will understand plain English,
> but jargon may puzzle them. My goal is simply to give them
> the information I would wish them to supply me if our posi-
> tions were reversed. To succeed, I don't need to be Shakespeare;
> I must, though, have a sincere desire to inform.
>
> No siblings to write to? Borrow mine: Just begin with
> "Dear Doris and Bertie."[9]

This advice from the CEO of Berkshire Hathaway, often referred
to as the Oracle of Omaha and considered one of the world's most astute investors, could have come straight out of a blogging handbook.

So, there's your easiest writing tip. Except it's not that easy to
write simply, concisely and clearly. I asked Noel Hartzell, executive
communications director for Sun Microsystems' Jonathan Schwartz,
why the COO's blog posts were so long. (They average 500 to 1,000
words.) Noel replied that Jonathan "wishes he had the time to be a

more crisp writer." To paraphrase Mark Twain, "I would have written a shorter letter but I didn't have the time."[10]

Bob Lutz's posts to GM's FastLane blog also average 500 words. According to GM's Michael Wiley, Lutz—if you can believe this—thumbs his blog articles into his BlackBerry and shoots them via email to Michael, who then pastes them into the blog. Michael swears that Bob's entries need almost no editing, even for typos or grammar.

The point is that while there is a rule of thumb for blogging (keep it short), you can do what you want. Better to post a long entry than not write anything at all. Note: You can, and should, use the "Continue to read more" link that's part of most blogging software. Just chop off your essay after 150 words or so and paste the rest into the "Continue" window. This way visitors to your blog page can skim a list of your most recent entries rather than be confronted with a daunting block of text.

If you're scratching your head at this point and wondering how you can write about a complex topic in an easy, conversational style, consider the following:

Ask yourself what William Strunk Jr. and E. B. White's classic *The Elements of Style* and Andrew Tobias's best-selling *The Only Investment Guide You'll Ever Need* have in common. They're written about serious, some might say dull topics—grammar and finance. You'll find them in the non-fiction section of the bookstore or library. And they're useful references you might want to consult again and again.

What they share: the two books are written in a graceful, conversational style. They're a pleasure to read. No choking on unfamiliar technical terms. No tortuously long sentences where you can't remember what the subject is by the time you get to the verb. You, the reader, are drawn into the story—and yes it can be a story whether the subject is proper grammar usage or the nitty-gritty of stocks and bonds and certificates of deposit. What's more, you can clearly hear the voices of these authors. You hear their quiet authority and the passion they have for their respective topics. You admire the clear thinking that translates the complex into the simple.

That's a hallmark of good blogging.

INVITE A CONVERSATION

This blog writing tip opens a can of worms for some corporate bloggers. If you "enable" the comments function on your blog it means that you are allowing readers to click and type in a comment. Thus you create a blog that's a conversation rather than a one-way publishing platform. I highly recommend that you do this. But what if the comments are negative? you ask. Or there are hundreds of them? Relax. Your challenge will most likely be to get readers to interact and leave any comments at all. The vast majority of blogs—corporate and personal—get few comments. Only a small number of blogs are popular enough to attract dozens or hundreds of comments in response to a single entry. (Bob Lutz's FastLane is one. Scott Adams's The Dilbert Blog is another. Go figure.)

Tip: there are several easy ways to manage reader comments. You can put them on a delay so that you have a chance to review the typed-in messages before publishing them yourself. This is a widely accepted practice. Another way to handle comments—and to prevent the growing amount of "comment spam" that blogs attract—is to configure your blogging program so that visitors must type in an illustrated "word" before submitting a comment. This prevents spambots from randomly trolling blogs and leaving unrelated and inappropriate messages on your blog.

YOUR WRITING FORMAT: PACKAGE WHAT YOU WRITE AND ALWAYS INCLUDE LINKS

Interestingly, the blog convention of short entries with links to other Web pages has its origins in the log-style Web site that was

Netscape's What's New page in the early 1990s. It was published daily from 1993 to 1996 and featured links to the best new sites with a snippet of description.[11] This style of blogging continues today, although blogging purists maintain that it's passionless, without opinion, and ultimately doesn't engage the reader.

As the *Wall Street Journal* put it, in a roundup of must-read blogs for insiders, "There are three basic varieties of blogs: those that post links to other sources, those that compile news and articles, and those that provide a forum for opinions and commentary. Some do one of these things or mix all three."[12]

Experiment and see what works for you. But always—always—include links in your blog entries. Links are the currency of the blogosphere. They're what determine a blog's popularity rating in Technorati. (The more links to your blog from other blogs, the higher your ranking. The idea is that what you're blogging about is important or useful or controversial enough that others freely reference it.) They're your way of connecting to the bigger conversation. And heck, link to your competitors. Link to other pages on your site. Link to Wikipedia or another reference to explain a term or source a quote. In other words, act a bit like a journalist. Don't be afraid that by inserting a link your reader will wander away and not come back to your blog. Everyone knows how to use the back button.

SHORT VERSUS LONG

Not to beat a dead horse, but a few more words on the short versus long question. It's foremost in the minds of most managers who are contemplating the launch of a company blog. How, oh how, to find the time to write the blog? I offered one suggestion in chapter 1: make blogging part of your daily habit of news gathering and sifting. Cull the links to articles you might want to blog about (I call these "bloggy bits") and paste them into the draft function of your blog software so you can come back later and type up an entry. Bloggable items are news stories related to your industry, links to downloadable surveys that have just been released (people love links to free stuff), or your commentary on something you've read on another blog.

Another approach is to codify your blogging approach in a Blogging Style Guide that you create for your blog writers. (Or ask your blog editor to create this.) Editor and content consultant Amy Gahran has identified and described seven ways of writing a blog post: a link-only; a link with a blurb; a brief remark; a list; a short article; a long article; a series. Each style serves a different purpose, she notes: "Consequently, some formats work best for commentary or explanation, others for alerts and references, etc."[13]

"In a perfect world I'd love to have another 5 to 10 hours a week to blog because I so enjoy it. Maybe I need a blog assistant. I have vast folders of stuff I could blog about."
—Denise Howell, Reed Smith
attorney and prolific blogger at
bgbg.blogspot.com

PACKAGING YOUR CONTENT INTO MANAGEABLE CHUNKS

A quick tip on how and why to do this. Make Top Ten lists (or top seven or top five). People love to read them. Other bloggers will link to them. Lists divide your blog entries into manageable sections. I titled this chapter a Top Ten for just that reason. There are probably 37 tips to write a good blog. But that's too many for you to wade through. Always write with an eye to your reader.

WRITE FOR WEB READERS AS WELL AS FOR GOOGLE

To write a blog is to write for the Web. Observe the following basic conventions and you'll develop more loyal readers:

- lots of white space

- snappy subheads

- bullets

- short paragraphs

- illustrations, whether photos, a graphic chart, or a video

In addition, take care with the title of your blog entry. It should be written to catch a reader's eye (remember, they may be reading the titles of your latest posts in an RSS newsreader). Make it specific and concrete. At the same time, write with an ear tuned to the search engines. For example, when I blogged about Bob Lutz and the FastLane blog, I tried to include both his name and General Motors in the title of an entry. Type "bob lutz gm blog" into Google and you'll see one of my blog entries from BlogWriteForCEOS.com, near the top of the page. Also be sure to include the kinds of keyword phrases in your entry that searchers might enter into Google. (For more on blog titles, see Jakob Nielsen's Weblog Usability tips in Bonus Resources.)

Here is an excellent list of specific suggestions to make your company blog a must-read online destination. Wrap it into your Blogging Style Guide as a reminder of how to slice and dice, present and package whatever topic you've chosen for your blog. With this many tips it will be hard to run out of ideas.

What Blog Readers Want to See More Of

by David Pollard

1. original research, surveys etc.

2. original, well-crafted fiction

3. great finds: resources, blogs, essays, artistic works

4. news not found anywhere else

5. category killers: aggregators that capture the best of many blogs/feeds, so they need not be read individually

6. clever, concise political opinion (most readers prefer these consistent with their own views)

7. benchmarks, quantitative analysis

8. personal stories, experiences, lessons learned

9. first-hand accounts

10. live reports from events

11. insight: leading-edge thinking & novel perspectives

12. short educational pieces

13. relevant "aha" graphics

14. great photos

15. useful tools and checklists

16. precis, summaries, reviews and other time-savers

17. fun stuff: quizzes, self-evaluations, other interactive content

What blog writers want more of:

1. constructive criticism, reaction, feedback

2. "thank you" comments, and why readers liked their post

3. requests for future posts on specific subjects

4. foundation articles: posts that writers can build on, on their own blogs

5. reading lists/aggregations of material on specific, leading-edge subjects that writers can use as resource material

6. wonderful examples of writing of a particular genre, that they can learn from

7. comments that engender lively discussion

8. guidance on how to write in the strange world of Weblogs.[14]

BLOGGING FREQUENCY

While it's ideal to post a new entry several times a week, sometimes it's just not possible. Don't, I repeat, don't let your latest month-old post sit there without an explanation. When you know you're going to take a break, post a short explanation for your hiatus and tell readers when to expect you back. Otherwise, it looks like you've abandoned your blog. Which defeats the purpose of creating a lively ongoing relationship with your audience.

TAKE RISKS

Talk about a controversial issue now and then. Go Daddy founder Bob Parsons does it regularly on his CEO blog. He loves to provoke a response and get dozens of comments back from readers. Bob has treaded into sensitive territory by opining about topics like Iraq and the U.S. policy on torture. I don't recommend either politics or religion as a topic. Too combustible. But your blog will get a lot of publicity if you're deliberately controversial. As more and more bloggers link to your entry—or to what others have said about it—you'll find your profile rising in blog search engines like Technorati and Blogpulse.

Sometimes you stir up a blogstorm by accident. That's what happened to Thomas Nelson CEO Michael Hyatt. Following the devastation of Hurricane Katrina in September 2005, he blogged about the publishing company's disaster relief plans. They included donating 100,000 bibles, which he had easy access to. Dozens of readers (83 in all) posted comments in response; many were highly critical. Michael published them all: "I felt that deleting them or filtering them would distort reality and make my blog less authentic. I also resisted the temptation to defend myself or my company, believing that my readers were doing an excellent job and it would be more compelling than me doing it."[15]

In other words, he didn't worry that the negative comments would sully his blog or his brand. While it's often true that you're defined by the company you keep, this is not the case on a blog. Your readers are smart. Trust them. They'll be impressed that you allowed contrarian views to remain part of your blog. And they'll make up their own minds about what to believe, depending on their outlook on the issue. Permitting, and publishing, critical feedback is part of the reason that blogging is messy, a term I used at the beginning of the chapter.

HAVE FUN

Yup. We're back to dancing. Bloggers who catch the bug like to write. They like to get feedback. They can stand the heat. They're often good writers, which is why their blog postings elicit a response. There's no reason a corporate blog can't develop the personality and flair of an individual's blog. After all, if you're doing it right your blog will have a distinctive voice. And perhaps a lead blogger for whom the blog is known. If you value cogent writing—and the passion and clear thinking behind it—and you embrace blogging as a new and sometimes unpredictable way to market, you're bound to have fun.

CHAPTER 8

What You Really Need to Know About Blogging Tools and Technology

Perhaps the coolest thing about blogging, and one of the major reasons the number of blogs is skyrocketing, is that the basic blogging tools are so easy to use. If you can compose and send an email via a Web-based service like Yahoo or Gmail, you can publish a blog. It's that simple. But dig a little deeper into the blogging tool chest and you'll come up with dozens of powerful accessories. These tech tools are often free and they're fun to use. More important, they're a necessity if you want to take full advantage of what the blogosphere has to offer you and your organization.

These tools and technologies range from specialized blog search engines, to the information-gathering and filtering capability of RSS (Really Simple Syndication, aka Web feeds), to new Web-based software that lets you collaborate in real time. You also need to become familiar with blogging's close cousins: tagging, podcasting and wikis.

If you're a geek, this is your chance to muck about with some cool applications. If you shun everything technical, take a deep breath. Now let it out. All you need to do is acquire a general understanding of the different kinds of blogging software, services and related tools—and what they can do for you. It's helpful to divide them into two categories:

1. blogging software: hosted versus in-house

2. RSS and other tools to sharpen your search and monitoring of the Web

Why is search important? Two reasons. First, you want efficient ways to search out information and resources to feed your own blog: other blogs and specific blog entries, links to articles, uploaded audio files or documents. Second, if your company doesn't have a corporate or official blog you still need to monitor what's being said about your brand, product or service in the blogosphere. Finally, if you do opt to launch your own blogging program, you want to increase the chances that your blog will get *found* by Web searchers and that you'll get the business results you're looking for. In other words, you want to maximize the marketing potential of your blog.

A third group of tools belongs in the "fun stuff to play with" category. Take a look at these when you have time or if you want to spiff up your blog with some cool features.

1. CHOOSING BLOGGING SOFTWARE: HOSTED VERSUS IN-HOUSE

Blogging software comes in two flavors: hosted, meaning your blog runs on a Web-based service and you concentrate on the creative and strategic end of blogging. And non-hosted—or in-house—meaning your blog is set up and maintained by your IT department. This requires some technical expertise including knowledge of advanced HTML, PHP, MySQL and other programming languages. (Don't ask me to elaborate.)

If you work for a large company, don't jump to the conclusion that you want your blog in-house. Corporate blogging is often a skunkworks project, an outside-the-box experiment. Run with that! If you're in a hurry, on a tight budget or just don't want to bother your IT department (i.e., get on their waiting list), using an outside service has a number of advantages. And yes, hosted blogs are secure. (Using a hosted blog service is no different from using an email service to deliver your e-newsletter.)

Hosted Blogging Software

To get started, you visit a site like TypePad.com, Blogger.com or WordPress.com and sign up for an account. Monthly fees for Type-Pad start at $5; Blogger and WordPress are free. At Blogger.com (owned by Google), you follow three steps:

1. Open a free account.

2. Name your blog (tip: stay simple and obvious).

3. Choose a template.

Presto! In minutes your blog is live on the Web. You can recognize blogs that are hosted on Blogger. They've got "blogspot" in the URL. Halley Suitt's blog, for example, resides at http://halleyscomment.blogspot.com. Bloggers all over the world use Blogger.com. The templates can be customized and spiffed up by a designer to look as cutting edge as you want.

Although it began as a service for individuals, many companies use TypePad as a hosted solution. It's owned by SixApart, one of the original blogging software companies. SixApart also makes the popular Movable Type, which is licensed software for installation. TypePad isn't a junior version of Movable Type, however. It's tricked out with every possible feature you need, and then some. You can add all the links and icons and photos you want in the left- or right-hand columns of the blog. The dynamic or changing text—with the most recent entry always at the top—is usually in the middle of the page. You can also publish multiple blogs through one TypePad account. With millions of users, TypePad encountered some serious difficulties in late 2005 when the service went down or ran slowly. SixApart promised to beef up capacity and speed, and planned to introduce a business-class version of the service.

For examples of TypePad blogs mentioned in this book, visit Air Conditioning Contractors of America's ACCABuzz at acca.blogs. com and Intuit's QuickBooks Online blog at quickbooks_online_blog.typepad.com.

There are many other low-cost hosted blogging services used by businesses and professionals, including BlogHarbor.com, Expression Engine.com, SquareSpace.com and WordPress.com (free). Popular consumer blogging services include LiveJournal.com, MSN Spaces and Yahoo! 360.

All the hosted blogging services have a WYSIWYG (what you see is what you get) interface. It enables you to easily add links and upload photos, illustrations or audio files. No technical expertise or programming knowledge is necessary.

In-House and Enterprise Blogging Platforms

If you're paranoid about security, want to integrate a large number of blogs with your intranet and/or want to do a significant amount of custom configuration, in-house blogging platforms can be a better solution. Popular choices include SixApart's Movable Type and the open source (i.e., free) and increasingly popular WordPress.org.

In addition, a new class of enterprise blogging platforms is emerging. "Enterprise" means—in plain-speak—that the software is tied into the organization's intranet. IBM, Sun and Microsoft have their own enterprise blogging systems. Content management systems like Domino and Stellent have blog and wiki templates. Enterprise blogging platforms you can license include iUpload, Socialtext and TractionSoftware.

State Farm's Hurricane Katrina Blogs

Still convinced that your IT department—or communications folks—will have a fit when you suggest adding multiple blogs to your intranet or public Web site? It may be easier than you think. Kelly Thul, a director of enterprise Internet solutions for State Farm, the world's largest auto insurer, was given the green light in early 2005 to launch up to 20 internal blogs. The goal was for the blogs to be an experiment in internal communications. He didn't get much resistance from top management, he told me, because clear plans were shared on how these blogs would be monitored.

Technically, it wasn't hard at all. State Farm uses IBM's Domino/Lotus Notes. It was simply a matter of adding Domino's blogging template. He assured the internal communications managers that the blogs would "not be a soapbox for employees" with gripes or concerns. But would be an informal way of communicating "to achieve certain goals."

Then Hurricane Katrina struck in August 2005. Thul and his team immediately launched two blogs (one for the Georgia and Mississippi region; one for Louisiana). Their purpose was specific: to find employees or insurance agents or their staff who were unaccounted for. State Farm's communications strategist for Georgia, Alabama and Mississippi took the lead on one of the blogs and began posting: "We're looking for some folks. Have you heard anything about them?"

The response was amazing, Thul said. The blogs enabled "people who *had* the information to connect with those who wanted the information." Within several days, almost everyone had been found. Thul, meanwhile, was getting updates to the blogs emailed to his BlackBerry. Each message that came in with news of someone being located was like a gift, he said.

The hurricane blogs are lying dormant for now. But about a

dozen other internal blogs have taken off, Thul said. Several are run by the IT department to discuss and manage projects. One is run by a group of State Farm communicators and writers. It discusses "big issues" like how to get the auto insurer's message across. None of the internal blogs are controversial or provocative, he said. But no matter. They're working.

The company had experimented for about ten years with discussion groups, but they never got "much traction," he said. They were too much like "a cocktail party where nobody is in charge and it can get noisy. A blog is closer to a radio show. They may take callers and comments; they may not." The key difference, Thul concluded, a blog has a producer and perhaps several editors who are responsible for keeping the show going.[1]

It should also be noted that you can publish multiple interconnected blogs through an outside hosting service. 21Publish and MyST Blogsite are two examples. Amnesty International USA publishes a handful of interconnected blogs at blogs.amnestyusa.org using 21Publish. Bill French, cofounder of MyST Technologies, explains that his blogsite platform is optimized to attract search engines and gain "greater Internet visibility for products, services, and company brands." It's also used internally by companies like Intel and Verisign.

You'll need to do your own due diligence to determine which blogging platform is right for you. Just *don't* let your IT department offer to build you a blogging solution from scratch. That's a complete waste of time and money. As you've just read, there are numerous existing options that are well tested and in wide use. And your IT folks can have plenty of fun adapting and customizing an open source blogging platform for your needs.

2. RSS AND OTHER TOOLS TO SHARPEN YOUR SEARCH AND MONITORING OF THE WEB

RSS Demystified

RSS is the single most important accessory to a blog. It's both a way to search the Web and create your own personalized news feed as well as a way to draw readers back to your blog again and again. Because of its confusing acronym (Really Simple Syndication) and the fact that you need a specialized newsreader[2] in order to subscribe to an RSS feed, its adoption rate has been slow.

In fact, RSS can be confounding to the uninitiated. A study by Yahoo and Ipsos Insight found that only 12 percent of Internet users were aware of RSS.[3] All you really need to know is that RSS is a means to publish and/or receive online news and information *without using email.* So, no spam filters blocking emails, no junk folders siphoning off messages.

Frankly, it's quite possible you'll never need to concern yourself with this geeky acronym. RSS or Web feed readers are being baked into Web browsers like Safari for the Mac and the popular Firefox. RSS is already part of My Yahoo! and Google's Gmail. And RSS will be seamlessly built into the next version of Microsoft's Internet Explorer. Oh, and you won't hear about RSS from Microsoft. They're planning to drop the acronym in favor of the term "Web feeds."

The important point is that RSS is just a channel, much as email is a channel. As RSS expert Rok Hrastnik puts it: blogs and e-zines are "the what" (the content) that you publish online; RSS and email are "the how" (the delivery mechanism).[4]

What (the content)	How (the delivery)
E-newsletters or e-zines	email and RSS
Blogs	RSS
News article	RSS
Status alerts	RSS
Product updates (whether it's the specific make and model of your car or your refrigerator)	RSS
New downloads	RSS
Updated asking price for houses in the neighborhood you want to move into	RSS
Latest movies at your closest theater	RSS
Lowest airfares to the Caribbean	RSS

In the long run, I predict that RSS will be more significant as a "channel" than email. It enables you to customize your use of the Web, whether you're *pushing* an RSS feed from your site or *pulling* in feeds on specific topics that you want to keep abreast of. Currently, RSS has some drawbacks as a publishing channel compared with email marketing. You can't apply precise metrics of open rates and click-throughs as you can with email marketing. This may not matter. End users are surfeited with email and, according to every study, tired of being bombarded with unsolicited messages. RSS is less intrusive (you don't have to divulge your email address to subscribe to a feed) and more customizable. As it becomes more intuitive to use, RSS will be ubiquitous.

RSS Explained

by Seth Godin

RSS is just a little peep, a signal, a ping that comes from a favorite blog or site, telling your computer that it has been updated. If you have an RSS reader (and they're free and easy, and two of the easiest live on the Web so you don't even have to install anything), whenever a blog is updated, it shows up in your reader and you can catch up on the news. If there's nothing new, it doesn't show up and you don't have to waste time surfing around.[5]

Using RSS to Publish News and Updates from Your Site

If you're wondering what kinds of companies are publishing RSS feeds from their sites, here's a random sampling: Oracle, Amazon, Microsoft, National Government of Canada, Cisco, Nokia, SAP, eBay, Apple Computer, AES Corporation, Center for Bioethics, United States Computer Emergency Readiness Team, Rhode Island Secretary of State, NOAA and Deloitte.

They're using RSS to publish everything from status alerts to press releases to information on new product releases. In fact, every possible specific topic you might want information on (your make and model of car, movies in your local theaters, best airfares to the Caribbean) can be delivered to you via RSS. You can slice and dice your content as thinly and precisely as you want. And create an RSS feed for each slice. *RSS feeds don't need to be connected to a blog.* One of the best uses for RSS on a corporate site is for the press or media page. Once reporters and editors are subscribed, they automatically get your latest news releases along with any other tidbits of information you push to them. IBM, Intel and lots of other corporations are already doing this.

Using RSS to Create Your Customized Search of the Web

Now comes the fun part. You can create multiple searches on keyword phrases and ask results to be delivered to you either in an email update—or via RSS. Steve Rubel, senior VP of the global PR firm Edelman and the prolific author of MicroPersuasion.com, told me he starts his blog publishing routine at 5 AM every morning.[6] First he scans over 300 blogs that he's subscribed to via RSS. Then, to aid in his search for news items on marketing, PR and technology, he uses Blogdigger, CNET's Newburst, Google News, IceRocket, Topix.net and Technorati. He has previously entered a list of words or keyphrases into each of these search services. His list includes variations on the common terms he's interested in. For example:

blog
blogs
blogger
bloggers
weblog
web log
weblogs
web logs

(Note: You can get Google News and other search results delivered to your desktop or other device via RSS or email.)

After scanning his many sources, he "picks the best stuff and gets it up on the blog early so it can reach European readers," he told me. He doesn't consider this kind of blogging as "writing." His posts are quick annotations of 100 to 150 words, or less. Only once a week does he take the time to write something longer. Why? "It takes more time and thought," he said.

Steve's approach points to the importance of having a "system" to collect fodder for your blog. As well as to the elastic notion of what blogging means. As we saw in chapter 7, blogging can mean a link with a brief explanation, a short paragraph or a long essay. It's your choice, or your lead blogger's choice. Just keep feeding the blog.

How to Monitor and Track What's Being Said About You

If you're in the preliminary stages of thinking about blogging, your first step is to play around with the blog search engines to monitor what's going on in the blogosphere that might relate to your brand, your products or services or your industry niche.

The main search engines are Technorati, Blogpulse, Feedster, Ice-Rocket and PubSub. Also Google Blog Search and Yahoo! News (which returns "blog" results as well as news stories when you search). They all work a little differently—and compile their lists of "most popular" blogs according to slightly different criteria. The best approach is to try searching each one for keyword phrases you're interested in. Or use an aggregator search engine like the nifty TalkDigger.com to get results back from all the top blog search engines. You'll quickly see that these specialized engines organize the results of your search in a number of ways: by most recent blog entries, by most influential blogs, by tags (more below on tagging) and even by trends. Blogpulse will create a trend chart of number of mentions of a certain phrase (your company name, for example). You can also create comparison trend charts for your brand versus your favorite competitor.

While you'll get a taste of what's being said about you in the blogosphere using these free tools, you'll soon find that your learnings are anecdotal at best. With more than 75,000 new blog entries being posted every day, it's hard to make sense of it all. So if you want to take a more serious step into blogosphere monitoring, you'll probably want to engage a specialized market research service to help. These include Buzz Metrics, Cymfony, Umbria Communications and IBM's Public Image Monitoring Solution. The services use sophisticated text-mining, data analysis and semantic search to find out—in nuanced terms—what's being said about your company throughout all forms of social media, including online discussion groups, opinion Web sites, Amazon and e-Bay reviews and blogs. Is it positive? Is it negative? Who's saying it—your employees, your customers?

Tagging

No explanation of blogging tools would be complete without mention of tagging. Here's a user-friendly explanation: tagging is an easy way of assigning keywords to your blog entries as well as to useful articles and resources you find online. You can also "tag" photos, using your name or an event or a trip, that you upload to the free Flickr. Sending a Flickr link is a wonderful alternative to sending an email when you want to point out specific blog entries, photos, news articles, etc.

A free service called del.icio.us is the ultimate tagging machine. Technorati, generally regarded as the leading blog search engine, also relies on tags to organize millions of blog entries. You can visit technorati.com and search on specific "tags." Tagging is part of a phenomenon called "social bookmarking," whereby we all collaborate to create a "folksonomy" of what's important. The best way to understand tagging, by the way, is to jump in and try it. Start with del.icio.us and Flickr.com.

BLOGGING'S CLOSE COUSINS: WIKIS AND PODCASTING

Wikis

Some are saying that email is out and collaborative wikis (editable Web sites) are in. Internet research firms like Gartner are predicting that "wikis will become mainstream collaboration tools in at least 50 percent of companies by 2009."[7] It's the same reasoning behind the rise of RSS as an alternative to email. Email messages are discrete, they clutter individual inboxes and they don't enable group collaboration. Wikis have been around for several years and often used internally. But until recently they required more programming skills than the average Web user possesses.

Companies like Socialtext, one of the leaders in the collaborative enterprise space, are changing that. For an example that builds on what we're covering in this book, take a look at the Fortune 500 Blogging Index. This is a group-edited wiki that tracks the increasing number of Fortune 500 blogs.[8] Another example is the popular wiki called Wikipedia, the volunteer-edited online encyclopedia. It was one of the top ten online news and information sites in November 2005.[9] As with all social media, you should maintain a healthy sense of skepticism about the veracity of information you find on a wiki. This is the beauty—and the beast—of consumer-generated media (CGM). CGM, estimated to comprise more than 50 percent of the content on the Web, is a rapidly expanding lode of information you can mine for opinions and insights. After all, CGM is what you use yourself when you go to buy a car, a digital camera or a flat-screen TV, right? You read customer reviews and recommendations. Then decide.

Podcasting

Blogs' other close cousin, in addition to wikis, are podcasts. It may seem puzzling at first that these downloadable audio files (they're like mini radio interviews) have anything to do with blogging. After all, they're audio content. The link is RSS. Just as you can subscribe via RSS to get the latest postings to a blog, you can subscribe via an RSS feed to have a podcast downloaded to your computer or your MP3 player of choice.

The term "podcast," of course, derives from Apple's ubiquitous iPod players. But you don't need an iPod to listen to a podcast. Any MP3 player will do. Podcast feeds are now seamlessly integrated with iTunes so it's easy to click and subscribe to the ones you want to hear.

And yes, corporations have jumped on podcasting as a new way to market and communicate. Companies from HP to IBM to Whirlpool are creating podcast shows on topics ranging from new technology forecasts to family issues. The best ones are like blogs—informal, non-salesy, even a bit quirky. And it's OK, even desirable, to have them sound a bit amateurish. That makes them more authentic.

What's really "new" about podcasts (after all, audio files have been available through the Web for years) is that they are transportable. Once you've downloaded a podcast, you can "unhook" from the Web and time shift. Listen to it in your car during your morning commute, on a jog or the exercise bicycle at your gym. Podcasts are emblematic of the new anytime, anywhere, any device Web. If you're thinking like a marketer, I can hear you salivate. Yes, this means that potentially you can follow your prospects and customers *wherever* they go with this new kind of content-based marketing collateral.

A FEW COOL TOOLS AND HACKS

Part of what distinguishes the so-called Web 2.0 is the proliferation of Web-based applications that use AJAX and other technologies to create collaborative tools. As examples take a look at 37signals.com and Google Maps. 37Signals makes Basecamp (for project management), Writeboard (a collaborative writing tool) and TagIt (an online To Do list). Another collaborative writing tool is Writely.com (now part of Google). You'll also want to use tools like Ecto to compose your blog entries offline.

Finally, if you want to embrace the customized, do-it-yourself nature of Web 2.0, you'll need to learn some hacks—i.e., clever ways of manipulating and combining online tools. This is beyond the scope of my expertise. But you can consult Steve Rubel's list of hacks for blogging, RSS, Technorati and Wikipedia.[10]

A Technorati Top 100 blogger, Steve publishes at Micro Persuasion.com on how new technologies are transforming marketing, media and public relations. His blogging hacks work on Blogger, TypePad and WordPress, he says, as well as most other blogging platforms.

They include:

- using Writely (writely.com) to blog alone or collaboratively. Also try Writely for any group writing project.

- Manipulating bookmarking site del.icio.us (type in del.icio.us) so that it automatically creates a new blog entry with your latest tagged links.

- Using ecto (ecto.kung-foo.tv) to automatically create Technorati tags.

If that's Greek to you, ask your nearest techie colleague to explain. You'll also need to check in with your geek friend on what the latest cool online tools are. No doubt there will be a raft of new ones by the time you read this.

CHAPTER 9

Cheat Sheet: Making the Case for Blogging to the Boss

If you're already blogging, perhaps the following scenario applies to you:

It's 5 AM. You've brewed a pot of coffee, and you're sitting at the kitchen table in front of your laptop (you've got WiFi, of course). You wake up slowly while skimming through the latest posts on your favorite 20 blogs. You like BoingBoing.net for serendipity. And Engadget.com because, well, you like tech stuff. You peruse a couple of blogs written by astute friends or colleagues. If you're a corporate manager, you skim blogs written by fellow execs or industry analysts or reporters from the *Wall Street Journal*, *Business-Week* or *Forbes*. Never know what tidbit you'll pick up. The reporters often offer up the backstory not included in their regular print columns. For a quick political fix, you take a look at Daily Kos.com (if you lean to the left) or Instapundit.com (if you lean to the right).

Thus fortified, you open up your own blogging program and type in a quick thought with your take on something you've just read. Or perhaps you drafted something at work yesterday when a new statistic or trend caught your attention. On the fly, you typed a note into your blog software and saved it in draft form, along with the links. Now you flesh out a couple of sentences or paragraphs, check your links, proofread, make a tiny edit or two . . . and publish.

Just another day in the blogosphere for you and millions and millions of others.

Except.

Except for your boss (or your board, if you're a CXX), who still hasn't gotten into this blogging thing or who doesn't really know what they are or how they work. Your boss who thinks blogs are a bunch of hot air, or too "soft" for business use. Your boss who isn't buying into an unproven communications fad.

Today's the day, you tell yourself. You're going to screw up your courage, marshal your facts, outline the business benefits, maybe spiff up your presentation in a PowerPoint and make the case for why your organization should start blogging.

On the other hand, maybe it's you who isn't quite there yet. You still have some reservations about this whole blogging thing, but your interest is piqued. You think blogs might be a valuable addition to your company's marketing strategy, and you can even envision how blogging might fit into your corporate culture. But you need just a bit more ammunition to make the case for blogging. You need the bullet points to outline the business benefits. And a quick step-by-step guide to get things going. (Note: This chapter primarily addresses public or external blogs. But you may want to review some of the points for internal blogging.)

Whichever scenario you fit into, this chapter is your cheat sheet. Let's start with a Rorschach test. Is this funny?

Question: How do you say blaa, blaa, blaa on the Internet?

Answer: Blog, blog, blog.

OK, just kidding about the Rorschach test. That's an old joke that made the rounds on the Internet several years ago. It puts bloggers in the category of self-indulgent whiners who keep online diaries or ne'er-do-wells who air their company's dirty laundry. If you've read this far, I hope you're a couple of steps beyond that point of view.

But perhaps you still want answers to some nagging questions. I've touched on these throughout the book but I want to come back to them. They're at the heart of the blogging phenomenon as it relates to business. They're the kinds of devil's advocate questions you should consider before approaching the rest of your team to make the case for blogging.

ASSESSING YOUR BLOGGING READINESS

Key Questions to Review	Answer
What problem does blogging solve?	Solves the "transparency and authenticity" issue bedeviling corporate America. Gives you an instant publishing channel to use any way you want.
What's the business case for blogging?	Although the ROB (return on blog) is soft, blogs are the perfect expression of FREE and fast. They give you a zero-transaction-cost way to connect with and learn from your customers (or employees). A public blog gives you high search engine rankings at little cost.
Why do we need to pay attention to the blogosphere?	You can ignore the blogviators. But listen to the influential blogs, interact with them and you'll be part of the new global conversation that's happening alongside MSM's version of events.

Key Questions to Review	Answer
What about credibility in the blogosphere?	Valid question. Beware. Unfortunately, half-truths spread quickly. Credible blogs will bubble up. Make your own a trusted resource.
How do we know if blogging is right for our organization?	Consider willingness to be open, whether you can add value with what you have to say, whether your company is in the eye of the media, whether you trust your employees to talk about your company, whether there is a need for trust in your brand, how a blog would mesh with other online content you are creating.

What Problem Does Blogging Solve?

Here's the off-the-cuff response. Authenticity. Transparency. Immediacy. Companies that publish blogs can help repair the public's damaged perception of corporate America, caused by the era of corporate malfeasance of the late 1990s. The Enrons and the Tycos and the Worldcoms, whose collapses personified corporate greed and hidden wrongdoing.

That's a grand idea and one I'd like to believe in. But I think the reality is much more prosaic—and more useful for your company. Blogs are an instant publishing channel. They circumvent the need to use mainstream media to get out your message. They enable a real-time connection with your customers. They're an unparalleled information-gathering mechanism that connects you with the buzz on whatever's being talked about. (Don't believe me? Go to Technorati. com and you'll see a list of the top ten hottest topics in the blogosphere. Usually, but not always, it correlates to what the top news of the day is. If it doesn't, pay attention. Maybe folks are stirred up about something that hasn't made it into the nightly news. Don't you want to be among the first to know?)

What Is the Business Case for Blogging?

The Web is where most people go first these days. Customers don't search for your company's number in the printed yellow pages, dial up your marketing department and ask to have your latest brochure mailed to them. I don't suppose you'd refuse to do this. But it's costly. Blogs, by contrast, give you a no-cost way to interact with— and get valuable feedback from—your audience, whether it's your customers, employees or other constituencies. Blogs are really and truly free. They're viral by nature, they're free spirited, they're free content. You give away this content if you're blogging yourself. Or consumers create it for you—free—if they're talking about your company or products.

What about the cost-benefit ratio, you ask. Blogging takes time. The ROI, or the ROB as we've called it, is soft. Yes, blogs represent a new branding and communications opportunity, but is that enough? Can you justify it? Writing in *BusinessWeek*'s Blogspotting.net blog, reporter Stephen Baker questioned whether spreading your "brand and message" really is the purpose of blogging. "I would argue that participating in the blog world is important for beat coverage. This is especially true in technology, media, design, advertising, and also perhaps in law and personal finance . . . My point . . . is that blogging is most important for what you learn."[1] I agree.

In addition, as we've discussed, a blog is a low-cost way to get high search engine rankings. Feed your blog regularly with relevant content. Watch it come up at the top of Google search results.

....

"Use this mnemonic:
BLOG stands for Better Listings on Google."
                                     —*Rick Bruner, Internet analyst*[2]

....

ONE MORE TIME, WHY DO WE NEED TO PAY ATTENTION TO THE BLOGOSPHERE?

There are thousands of droning, long-winded blogs. Indeed, they make up a good chunk of the din and chaos that is the blogosphere. That's not the part of the blogosphere you need to pay attention to. There's a self-correcting mechanism at work. Boring blogs don't get read or linked to. Thus they have little or no influence. The influential blogs tend to be the ones that make the Top 100 and Top 500 lists. Thousands of other bloggers are linking to and citing from these blogs. These are the blogs you need to listen to, to interact with by leaving a comment, or by emailing the blog publisher privately. These are the blogs that connect you to the "global conversation" that you've been hearing about. This "people's conversation" is assuming increasing importance as a trusted alternative to the version of events presented on nightly network news.

OK, but What About the Credibility of This "Global Conversation"?

Credibility is evolving as a key issue in the blogosphere. You're right to ask the question and right to be concerned. Every time a group of bloggers jumps on an issue or incident, talks it up, and sends it racing around the blogosphere it's perfectly valid to ask, "But is this really true?"

We saw that with the Kryptonite blogstorm. Bloggers assumed that the company had its head in the sand and wasn't paying attention to what the blogosphere was saying about the vulnerability of its bike locks. While the story is not a black and white one, it turned out that Kryptonite's PR manager was well aware of what the blogosphere was saying about the company's "cluelessness." But she was too busy to respond because she and the rest of the lockmaker's small staff of 25 were working around the clock to arrange the logistics of a free lock exchange.

The credibility of the blogosphere is lowered a couple of notches every time an erroneous meme like this spreads and takes root. It's happening in part because citizen journalists are just that—"amateur" journalists. I don't believe that they're mean spirited. Or that they're the "online lynch mob" that *Forbes* magazine called bloggers in a cover story.[3] It's just that they're in a rush to be the first to publish or comment on whatever the hot story is. So they omit the steps of attributing sources, double-checking facts, submitting copy for review by an editor—the old-fashioned best practices used by MSM journalists.

When I interviewed Kryptonite's Donna Tocci, she told me that not one single blogger called her to check out what was happening before blogging their version of the story. In contrast, she said, MSM reporters and editors were on the phone with her from Day One of the incident.

So How Do We Know if Launching Our Own Blog Is Right for Our Organization?

There is no clear-cut answer, but here are questions that can help you decide:

- Can you regularly update a blog—preferably several times a week?

- Do you have a writer or a group of writers to feed the blog?

- Do you have something to say other than just linking to other blogs or news sources?

- Can you provide information of value to your readers?

- Do you read other blogs and have a sense of what's being talked about relative to your industry, product or service?

- Do you have existing content on your Web site (white papers, articles, FAQs) that the blog could link to in order to draw visitors deeper into your main Web site?

- In other words, can you marry a blog with your existing online content so that you get more leverage out of your current site?

The "is blogging right for us" question demands serious reflection. You need to justify the time, creativity and passion involved in keeping an effective blog going. PR firm Waggoner Edstrom has devised an online Blogging Index that prompts you to consider additional factors.[4] It includes the following points:

1. My organization/division is willing to be transparent (open and authentic).

2. We have a unique perspective to offer the marketplace.

3. There is a significant need for trust in our brand before customers will buy it.

4. We need to build a stronger sense of loyalty and connection with our constituents.

5. Our product/brand category is going through significant change right now.

6. Our products have a long purchasing cycle and/or significant decision criteria.

7. Our product distribution is contingent upon third parties (e.g., the channel).

8. We manage issues/crises on a frequent basis.

9. Our company is high profile (frequently talked about in the media and with key constituents).

10. We trust our employees to talk openly about the company.

I suggest that you fill out the online form yourself. Tally the results and incorporate them into your blogging memo.

How Much Will It Cost and Do We Need a Consultant or an Agency to Help Us?

First, the cost of blogging is negligible for a large company, compared to other marketing communications strategies. The cost of the technology is close to zero, no matter which option you choose. The ongoing cost is one of managing and feeding the blog. By managing I mean monitoring the comments and trackbacks to the blog. By "feeding" I mean creating fresh content—i.e., writing the blog.

No doubt you're already publishing other information products—e-newsletters, white papers, articles, executive speeches, FAQs and other informational pages on your Web site. You may be able to assign management of the blog to the internal editor who is responsible for these other forms of content. Just be sure this person—or team—has a keen sense for PR and understands the two-way, conversational nature of a blog.

As Laurie Mayers, senior vice president of Hass MS&L, the agency that supports GM's FastLane blog, put it: "It's not absolutely necessary to have an agency's help, but a big company does need a focused team, either internal or external, that has done extensive research and reading of blogs. The team needs to be committed to communicating openly, willing to take considered risks, and needs to have good PR instincts."

If you choose to use an agency, it could be involved with "either monitoring or strategy, or both" Laurie suggested, noting that Hass MS&L does both for General Motors on the FastLane blog. "We moderate all the comments (about 6,000 of them so far) and trackbacks and monitor what people are saying elsewhere about the blog . . . We know what people are talking about, so we can help suggest topics for future posts or other ideas."

Working with an agency is a balancing act. If you're going to use one, you can lean on them for counsel. But they probably shouldn't write the blog for you. As Laurie put it, "The agency's role is not to tell the company exactly what to say in its blog. If an executive really doesn't want to talk about union difficulties or the share price, these issues are of such fundamental importance to the company that the agency should step out of the way. But it is part of the agency's responsibility to urge the company to discuss these and other relevant matters as openly as possible."[5]

Who Should Write a Corporate Blog?

In some ways, this is the most important question. Your blogger, whether hired or in-house, needs to be a good writer: authoritative, newsy yet informal. He or she should have a point of view that meshes with your company's, understand how to engage with the blogosphere, know how to respond to criticism, have the commitment and stamina to continue indefinitely—and be passionate about blogging.

"In a corporate sense, the more racy and immediate a blog, the less you can allow it to speak for your corporation. There's a lot of potential power, but risk-managing a blog seems to me to be a contradiction in terms."

—David Redhill, chief marketing officer of Deloitte Australia, as quoted in The Sydney Morning Herald, *August 16, 2005*

Some obvious suggestions for who might write your corporate blog:

- a senior exec who likes to write and can represent the face of your company

- a blog editor who either writes the blog him- or herself or solicits submissions from other staff members

Other ideas:

- Hire a blogger whose style and passion you admire and whose expertise fits with the topic you've chosen for your blog. It's best to let this person remain relatively independent. Of course, he or she should understand and adhere to whatever blogging guidelines you've created (see chapter 3) and be willing to represent your company's point of view as appropriate.

- Create a blogging channel. This means syndicating a handful of other blogs on topics relevant to your company or industry niche. Often the bloggers will be so delighted to get exposure to a wider audience that you won't need to pay them. (Remember, free and open and sharing are part of the blogging ethos. Take advantage of it.)

Syndicating means setting up a blog page on your site and using RSS to pull in the latest entries from your guest bloggers as feeds. Generally, one sees only the most recent entries. Included is a photograph and brief description of each blogger. Note that you can change the look and feel of the blogs so that they mesh with the design of your site.

Choosing a Lead Corporate Blogger with the Right Stuff

In any event, no matter who you choose to be your lead corporate blogger, there are some intangibles that must be satisfied in order for your blog to be a success. Richard Edelman, a respected CEO blogger, put it like this, writing on his blog[6]: "The primary skill must be an ability to connect in the blogosphere." He likens this ability to that of Bill Clinton—how he "made you feel in his presence, looking at you directly in the eye, asking questions, excited by your response, offering an unexpected view. The overused word charisma is very appropriate in this context."

The other piece of "connecting" is that the blogger needs to be a really good listener. Wrote Edelman, "It is clear that major companies should have 'specific skills bloggers' who can blog reliably and credibly in their areas of expertise. The technical bona fides are critical to the credibility of the blog, but not sufficient to attract long-term readership and participation. The blogger must be sensitive to what people want to hear, not just what he or she wants to write about."

In other words, your lead blogger should be a conduit, pulling in reaction and opinion and ideas from readers as much as he or she is broadcasting her own messages. Again, Edelman gets this spot on. From the same blog entry: "Smart marketers are looking at the blogosphere as a wonderful opportunity to ask for the wisdom of the crowd and . . . great companies are willing to offer the opportunity for co-creation of brands and corporate reputation."

PUTTING TOGETHER YOUR BLOGGING PITCH (HINT: CREATE A TEST BLOG)

We've covered just about every issue, hurdle and concern you might have about blogging. Now it's time for the pitch to your boss and/or to your team. But first, lay the groundwork:

1. Read 20 blogs and have the links handy to pass on to your coworkers or boss.

2. Subscribe to the blogs via the RSS reader of your choice.

3. Create a test blog and fill it with some relevant content. In other words, do some blogging yourself even if you won't be the designated blogger in the long run.

4. Set up a meeting with your boss to show him how the test blog works and how easy it is to add an entry that includes links, photos, etc. Show him or her how the RSS reader works.

5. Have answers prepared to some of the most commonly asked questions: Who will write the company blog? What results will we get out of it? How hard will it be to maintain? Won't Legal have a fit?

How to set up a test blog

The best way to educate your boss—or to get yourself up to speed—on how blogging works is to start a blog. I recommend that you spend the better part of a day on this. Yes, you can open a free Blogger.com account in minutes. But I suggest you choose a more full-featured blogging solution. TypePad.com is a good choice (and usually offers a 30-day free trial). As we learned in chapter 8, you can add lots of bells and whistles (lists of resources, images, icons to prompt subscribing to the blog) in the left- and right-hand columns. It's worth taking the time to do this because it illustrates the different things a blog can do and also shows how your blog links back to and ties into your main Web site.

(You can also set up a blog in TypePad so that it is private and password protected. You can change this later if you decide to go public.)

Name Your Blog

You'll need to do this anyway to set up your blogging account. Here's a tip: don't get too creative. In fact, use your company name. Remember that one of your goals is to get high search engine rankings. If you use Blogger.com, your blog will be at your company.blogspot.com. If you use TypePad, your URL will look like this: yourcompany.typepad.com or yourcompany.blogs.com. You want someone typing in the name of your company, brand or product to stumble onto your blog in search results.

Another way to choose a name for your blog is to register a separate URL. In other words, see what domain names are available and choose a blog name that way. (Even if you set up your test blog on blogger.com or typepad.com, you can always have it resolve to this URL later.)

Create Categories and Add a Few Entries

You'll want to choose a template and a color scheme to make your test blog match your site. Just as important, you need to set up half a dozen "categories" (blog lingo) on topics that you think the blog will cover. Then be brave and type in a few entries. Assign each entry to a different category. Add some "comments" (blog lingo) yourself. Or get a colleague to type in some comments on what you've written. Don't fret over the advice you've gotten thus far on how to perfect a bloggy voice, etc. Just make something up. Or get a creative colleague to do the writing.

If you're scratching your head as to what your categories should be, go look at some other blogs for ideas. In fact, keep your browser open the whole time you're setting up your test blog so you can look at other blogs for ideas. (See TheCorporate BloggingBook.com for direct links to recommended blogs.)

The reason you need to create categories and add comments is so that you can show how the content management function of the blog works during your live demo. In other words, you can demo how the blog slices and dices content by date or by topic. How each entry is enriched by comments left by readers and so on.

OK, you're ready. You've met with your boss, coached him or her on how blogging works and gotten the go-ahead to pitch a blogging program to the whole team. Consult the chart for what points to cover. Review the following "blogging memo" put together by GM's

Michael Wiley. As you'll see, he touches on the key points: why a blog, how it will work, what results to expect.

What to Include in Your Blogging Pitch

1. The goal of your blog

2. Who will write it and who will manage it

3. Suggested Corporate Blogging Guidelines (see samples in Bonus Resources)

4. What business results to expect (explain the importance of CGM [consumer generated media] and learning from your customers)

5. Cost estimates and logistics to maintain the blog

6. Unveil your test blog with a live demo (you'll need online access)

7. Easy next steps to launch (explain that the test blog can be tweaked and go live!)

How to Write "the Blogging Memo"

Nothing easier than cribbing from someone else's memo, right? This one was short and sweet—and effective. It successfully made the case for launching GM's FastLane blog in January 2005.[7] Here are the verbatim bullet points from the Executive Summary PowerPoint slide prepared by Michael Wiley, GM's director of Internet Marketing:

Why Launch GM FastLane?

- Opportunities exist for a direct line of communication, a "cleaner" information voice to both consumers and employees.

- Media coverage is filtered.

- FastLane Blog should be launched in January to build interest in the new Saturn model lineup introduced at the Detroit Show.

Principles of Operation

- Company position but candid and transparent,

- Engage in two-way conversation with constituencies,

- Eventually spread the voice beyond hard-core bloggers and car buffs

Expected Results

- FastLane will position GM as forward-thinking and willing to take risks. Our willingness to accept negative feedback will promote an image of transparency and accountability.

- FastLane will be featured as a prototype for grassroots communication in press reports covering this burgeoning movement. [Note: this was a good call on Michael's part as this is exactly what happened!]

- FastLane will further position Bob Lutz as a visionary leader.

You're done! I hope you get the green light for your corporate blog. And that your designated blogger(s) dive in and just do it.

CHAPTER 10

What's Next

This book stands on the premise that blogging has not been over-hyped. It's not a fad. It's a new communications tool—in fact a whole new arena of marketing—that every businessperson needs to become conversant with, if not fluent in. If you're a CEO or senior executive, a blog offers you a remarkably efficient way to communicate intelligently with a lot more people, which is after all, a key part of your job. If you're a product manager in a Fortune 500, blogging is a new way to connect with and learn from your customers. A blog can be quicker, more revealing—and certainly more cost effective—than focus groups. If you're a solopreneur or a microenterprise, a blog is your dream marketing machine. Entrepreneur and blogger David St. Lawrence calls it "the ultimate power tool available to a single individual. It provides almost unlimited multiplication of effort."[1]

So what does the future hold for corporate blogging? Well, for starters the blog explosion is beginning to quiet down. By now hundreds of thousands of blogs—business and personal—have died a natural death. "It's Darwinism," explained Pat Cleary, author of the National Association of Manufacturers' blog. "Good blogs will survive and bad ones will fall by the wayside." And some good bloggers will tire and stop blogging. Granted, many of the best blogs are not going to be corporate; that is, blogs published by big companies. The smartest, most provocative blogs tend to be published by individuals—whether it's Dilbert creator Scott Adams at dilbert blog.typepad.com or the curmudgeonly Hugh Macleod at gaping void.com, one of the best-read blogs in Europe.

"Blogs are no fad. They are cheap and easy to do. And blogs fulfill that deepest of human needs as defined by psychologist Abraham Maslow: self-actualization. People write blogs because they want to know themselves and want to be known by others and because they want their lives to count. When a communications medium is . . . tapping into a deep need, it's no fad."

—Rich Karlgaard, publisher of Forbes *magazine, on his blog, December 26, 2005*

I predict that corporate blogs will stake out their own corner of blogdom. They will define a slice of the blogosphere where the rules, perhaps, are a bit more forgiving and where edginess isn't the most important feature. Many big company blogs will be a bit more sedate, a lot less controversial—and possibly less engaging. They will, in short, become a new form of marketing vehicle that may or may not remain true to the original spirit of blogging. But if you employ some of the best practices I've outlined for how to write your blog in a friendly human voice, for how to muster equal parts passion and authority to connect with your readers, and for how to really listen, you are going to get a ROB that will make the effort worth it.

Your regular readership doesn't need to be a huge one, by the way. It just needs to be representative of the customers you're trying to market to. Which, no matter how big your consumer brand is, is not going to be everybody. In any case, unless your service is a Web-based one where, by definition, your customers are online in order to use it, not everyone in your target market is going to interact with your blog. Here is where the Long Tail comes in.[2] The Long Tail is a concept that buzzed around the blogosphere in 2005. It refers to the millions of tiny niche markets along the skinny tail of the demand curve (think back to your economics class or see squidoo.com/longtail for a more complete explanation and an illustration). Until recently, these little markets were considered too small to pay attention to. The sensible bet for most big businesses was to pay attention to the high end of the demand curve where, traditionally, your biggest market of one-size-fits-all customers clustered. (And where mass market advertising made sense because that was the best way to reach those people.)

"Blogging is a symptom of something much bigger that's happening."

—*Dave Sifry, CEO, Technorati*

But blogging is tailor-made for the Long Tail. The blogosphere, a fragmented market if ever there was one, *is* the Long Tail. What this means for you is that it doesn't matter if your company blog, or your employees' blogs, make it onto the Technorati Top 100 or the Feedster Top 500 lists. (One of the very few examples of a single such influential employee blog is Microsoft's Robert Scoble and his scobleizer.com.) What's important is that your blog engage the specific audience you want to have a conversation with. That might be millions of people if your market is coffee drinkers. (If that is the case, pick a unique niche within the topic of coffee drinking. Say, home brewing. Otherwise your blog won't stand out.) On the other hand, it might be only hundreds, or perhaps thousands, of potential readers if your market is a specialized business-to-business one like RFID (radio frequency identification) products for, er, gas stations. Those things you wave in front of the gas meter.

The blogosphere that counts—the one you need to concern yourself with as a businessperson—is the collection of *influential* blogs that talk back and forth to one another, creating the biggest global echo chamber we've ever known. Yes, the total count of blogs worldwide approaches 100 million as you read this. But the number of blogs that make up the blogosphere you should pay attention to is far smaller, numbering perhaps in the thousands.

The echo effect is key. It's a wonderful thing if you're on the inside, you're blogging and you're being linked to and cited and you're linking out and referring to other blogs. You feel like you belong. Your readers (even if it's only several hundred a day, as is the case for the QuickBooks Online blog) nod appreciatively at your entries and may find them useful. But if you're on the outside and suddenly you get picked on, as bike lockmaker Kryptonite experienced, the blogosphere can be a painful place.

The lesson here is "pay attention." You may still be thinking that blogging has nothing to do with your business. But it just might, given the unpredictable nature of bloggers and of the topics du jour that race around the blogosphere with sometimes frightening speed. The instant amplification of the blogosphere—which happens when the influential bloggers are listening and their ears prick up—can't be stressed enough. Use it to your advantage. Get inside this global echo chamber.

CITIZEN JOURNALISTS AND CITIZEN MARKETERS

Just as blogging has enabled a whole new generation of citizen journalists, those smart observers who pick up tidbits overlooked by mainstream media and publish immediately, without the constraints of network news cycles or editors looking over their shoulders, so citizen marketers are redefining who is doing the selling for your company. They create fan blogs, upload homemade videos (remember the flying iPods?), download the Firefox Web browser (24 million downloads in three months) and otherwise *do the work for you*. As author Jackie Huba put it:

In many cases, citizen media is more authentic and believable than agency work. It's created by customers not schooled in the traditional means of advertising . . .

Citizen marketers aren't required to overlook problems or mask shortcomings. But they may offer a workaround. Or justification for a feature or service some may consider wrong or shortsighted . . .

Citizen marketing is produced without the benefit of expense accounts, big budgets or pajama-clad creative directors . . . Citizen marketing is more believable and impactful than the stuff being produced for mass media today. Their creative work is based on their intimate knowledge of the product, thereby making it authentic.[3]

And where do these citizen marketers do their work? In the Long Tail of the blogosphere, of course. Embrace them. Heed them. Consumer-generated media, as we learned in chapter 8, is far more trusted than traditional advertising. According to Edelman's 7th Annual Trust Barometer, trust in a person "like me" has risen from 20 percent in 2003 to 68 percent today.[4]

"The word PR will be gone. The word blog will be gone. Your employees will be your ad agency. And your customers will be your backup ad agency."

—blogger Halley Suitt

WEB 2.0 AND THE NEW BUSINESS ECOSYSTEM

Which brings us to another piece of the "what's next" puzzle. Web 2.0 is a made-up term to conjure up the next generation of the Web. It describes an online experience that's more user-friendly and more useful. You'll experience it through user-generated content (blogging is one example), easy-to-use collaborative tools (wikis are an example but they're not "new") and the ability to customize your use of the Web. In other words, the Web as "firehose" of information blasting at you indiscriminately (when you type a word into Google and get 23 million results, for example) will be transformed into your personal "straw" where you suck up just what you want, when you want. And yes, you'll be using customized Web feeds (RSS) to do this.

That's why podcasts are significant. They're little slices of audio content, created by thousands of individuals—and some companies—that you can listen to at your convenience. (Again, the Long Tail.) If you're creating podcasts (which are a no-brainer analog to publishing a blog), you can follow your customers wherever they go.

People are calling this a new business ecosystem. The best stuff is bubbling up from below. And I don't just mean new business ideas or new products. Often, the best writing and thinking can be found on blogs. Blogging goes way beyond a new business tool or communications channel. Self-publishing is revolutionizing the way we consume news and information, make purchase decisions, travel and learn.

As Thomas Friedman puts it in *The World Is Flat,* individuals are as much a part of the supply chain "flattening" the world economy as businesses are. The Internet has enabled a frictionless way of doing business. It has flattened the world economy and made it a level playing field for everyone, no matter what size your company or organization or whether you're in a first- or third-world country. You've heard of outsourcing. Friedman has invented the term "in-forming."

Blogging Is Part of "In-forming"
by Thomas L. Friedman[5]

....

*"In-forming is the individual person's analog to open-sourcing,
outsourcing, insourcing, supply-chaining, and offshoring. In-
forming is the ability to build and supply your own personal
supply chain—a supply chain of information, knowledge, and
entertainment. In-forming is about self-collaboration—
becoming your own self-directed and self-empowered researcher,
editor, and selector of entertainment . . . Google's phenomenal
global popularity . . . shows how hungry people are for this form
of collaboration. Google is now processing roughly one billion
searches per day, up from 150 million just three years ago."*

....

THE FUTURE OF AUTHENTICITY

Will corporate blogs become a slick new media, a form of advertor-
ial, that loses the rawness and realness that defines blogging? I
don't have the answer. But I hope not. The best corporate blogs
share a lot of the characteristics of the best media sites. These
blogs tell stories. They're well written. They make you hungry for
the next installment. They're authentic-sounding enough that you
begin to form a relationship with the authors, whether it's Sun
Microsystems' Jonathan Schwartz or J. D. Iles of Lincoln Sign
Company.

Corporate-Speak Is Dead

by Peter Hirshberg, Executive VP of Technorati

The nature of corporate communication will change. The voice
will change. Fifty years of highly structured corporate-speak,
of words that are poured over by teams of marcom and PR

people will go away in favor of immediacy, plain talking and authenticity. It's not that corporate blogs will take off, it's that marketers will learn from bloggers how to speak in a human voice and this will show up in Websites, in print advertising and on TV.

Current corporate-speak is a remnant of one-way mass communication. It's stilted, just as a soliloquy in Shakespeare seems stilted. Conversations are not speeches and soliloquies. As the audience and the customer become part of a two-way communication, corporations will learn to speak like people.[6]

Go take a look at the big-dog bloggers I've mentioned in previous chapters. A sample listing: Boeing, General Motors, Hill & Knowlton, HP, Intuit, Macromedia, Sun Microsystems. And some of the smaller business blogs: SignsNeverSleep, e-tailer BlueFly, 800-CEO-Read, Stonyfield Farm, Seth Godin. Which of these is still going strong? Which looks like good reading, and not just an occasional perfunctory post? Which looks like an editorial model you might copy from? For example, CEO blogger, hired editor, knowledgeable employee, passionate customer?

IT'S NOT ABOUT BEING COOL

Now before you snap this book closed and say oh that's all very well and good. Sounds exciting and kinda interesting but my company would *never* get into blogging. Too much time, too much work, not yet proven . . . consider the following:

This is not about being cool. This is about where everyone is going—online. This is where your customers will be soon, if they're not there already. According to the Pew Internet & American Life Project, 3 percent of online seniors are blogging. In contrast, 57 percent of teenagers who use the Internet have created a blog, uploaded photos, audio or video or remixed online content to create new stuff.[7] Their lives are inextricably intertwined with the online world.

Increasingly, the new marketing—whether it's blogging or podcasting or vlogging (video blogging)—overlaps with our consumption of news and entertainment. Corporate blogging done right should not feel like a marketing experience. It should come across as the inside story, the pulse, the personality of your company.

Here is where I leave you, somewhat reluctantly. The story of corporate blogging is still unfolding. I'd like to tie it up neatly for you. But in true blogging style, I can't. There's always another entry, a new tidbit, more feedback from readers. (Remember, I want to hear from you!) But you've got more than enough information to jump in. Heck, you're already in the race if you're reading this book.

Go make it happen. Have fun. Life is short. It's also messy and wonderful. Like blogging.

Bonus Resources

SAMPLE BLOGGING POLICIES AND GUIDELINES

The sample policies and guidelines that follow are ones you can base your own company's blogging prescription on. I've chosen these because they are examples that encourage and at the same time circumscribe blogging as a communications tool for employees. They point out both advantages and pitfalls in clear, non-legalese.

IBM Blogging Policy and Guidelines

IBM was one of the first companies to make its blogging guidelines publicly available. A short introduction puts blogging in the broader context of IBM's "responsible involvement" in the new collaborative business ecosystem. While blogging as an IBM employee is encouraged, the guidelines make it clear that the blogger is personally responsible for what he or she publishes. You can download the complete guidelines, including Detailed Discussion, from www-128.ibm.com/developerworks/blogs/dw_blog_comments.jspa?blog=351&entry=81328.

Responsible Engagement in Innovation and Dialogue

Whether or not an IBMer chooses to create or participate in a blog or a wiki or other form of online publishing or discussion is his or her own decision. However, it is very much in IBM's interest—and, we believe, in each IBMer's own—to be aware of this sphere of information, interaction and idea exchange:

To learn: As an innovation-based company, we believe in the importance of open exchange and learning—between IBM and its clients, and among the many constituents of our emerging business and societal ecosystem. The rapidly growing phenomenon of blogging and online dialogue are emerging important arenas for that kind of engagement and learning.

To contribute: IBM—as a business, as an innovator and as a corporate citizen—makes important contributions to the world, to the future of business and technology, and to public dialogue on a broad range of societal issues. As our business activities increasingly focus on the provision of transformational insight and high-value innovation—whether to business clients or those in the public, educational or health sectors—it becomes increasingly important for IBM and IBMers to share with the world the exciting things we're learning and doing, and to learn from others.

In 1997, IBM recommended that its employees get out onto the Net—at a time when many companies were seeking to restrict their employees' Internet access. We continue to advocate IBMers' responsible involvement today in this new, rapidly growing space of relationship, learning and collaboration.

Guidelines for IBM Bloggers: Executive Summary

1. Know and follow IBM's Business Conduct Guidelines.

2. Blogs, wikis and other forms of online discourse are individual interactions, not corporate communications. IBMers are personally responsible for their posts. Be mindful that what you write will be public for a long time—protect your privacy.

3. Identify yourself—name and, when relevant, role at IBM— when you blog about IBM or IBM-related matters. And write

in the first person. You must make it clear that you are speaking for yourself and not on behalf of IBM.

4. If you publish a blog or post to a blog outside of IBM and it has something to do with work you do or subjects associated with IBM, use a disclaimer such as this: "The postings on this site are my own and don't necessarily represent IBM's positions, strategies or opinions."

5. Respect copyright, fair use and financial disclosure laws.

6. Don't provide IBM's or another's confidential or other proprietary information. Ask permission to publish or report on conversations that are meant to be private or internal to IBM.

7. Don't cite or reference clients, partners or suppliers without their approval.

8. Respect your audience. Don't use ethnic slurs, personal insults, obscenity, etc., and show proper consideration for others' privacy and for topics that may be considered objectionable or inflammatory—such as politics and religion.

9. Find out who else is blogging on the topic, and cite them.

10. Don't pick fights, be the first to correct your own mistakes, and don't alter previous posts without indicating that you have done so.

11. Try to add value. Provide worthwhile information and perspective.

Sun Microsystem's Policy on Public Discourse

Sun's policy is notable for the fact that it's couched in informal terms and is written much as an experienced blogger might write to a newbie, offering morsels of advice. Note the emphasis on what to write about as well as how. This policy is published online at sun.com/aboutsun/media/blogs/policy.html.

Many of us at Sun are doing work that could change the world. We need to do a better job of telling the world. As of now, you are encouraged to tell the world about your work, without asking permission first (but please do read and follow the advice in this note). Blogging is a good way to do this.

Advice   By speaking directly to the world, without benefit of management approval, we are accepting higher risks in the interest of higher rewards. We don't want to micro-manage, but here is some advice.

It's a Two-Way Street   The real goal isn't to get everyone at Sun blogging, it's to become part of the industry conversation. So, whether or not you're going to write, and especially if you are, look around and do some reading, so you learn where the conversation is and what people are saying.

If you start writing, remember the Web is all about links; when you see something interesting and relevant, link to it; you'll be doing your readers a service, and you'll also generate links back to you; a win-win.

Don't Tell Secrets   Common sense at work here; it's perfectly OK to talk about your work and have a dialog with the community, but it's not OK to publish the recipe for one of our secret sauces. There's an official policy on protecting Sun's proprietary and confidential information, but there are still going to be judgment calls.

If the judgment call is tough—on secrets or one of the other issues discussed here—it's never a bad idea to get management sign-off before you publish.

Be Interesting   Writing is hard work. There's no point doing it if people don't read it. Fortunately, if you're writing about a product that a lot of people are using, or are waiting for, and you know what you're talking about, you're probably going to be interesting. And because of the magic of hyperlinking and the Web, if you're interesting, you're going to be popular, at least among the people who understand your specialty.

Another way to be interesting is to expose your personality; almost all of the successful bloggers write about themselves, about families or movies or books or games; or they post pictures. People like to know what kind of a person is writing what they're reading. Once again, balance is called for; a blog is a public place and you should try to avoid embarrassing your readers or the company.

Write What You Know   The best way to be interesting, stay out of trouble, and have fun is to write about what you know. If you have a deep understanding of some chunk of Solaris or a hot JSR, it's hard to get into too much trouble, or be boring, talking about the issues and challenges around that.

On the other hand, a Solaris architect who publishes rants on marketing strategy, or whether Java should be open-sourced, has a good chance of being embarrassed by a real expert, or of being boring.

Financial Rules   There are all sorts of laws about what we can and can't say, business-wise. Talking about revenue, future product ship dates, roadmaps, or our share price is apt to get you, or the company, or both, into legal trouble.

Quality Matters   Use a spell-checker. If you're not design-oriented, ask someone who is whether your blog looks decent, and take their advice on how to improve it.

You don't have to be a great or even a good writer to succeed at this, but you do have to make an effort to be clear, complete, and concise. Of course, "complete" and "concise" are to some degree in conflict; that's just the way life is. There are very few first drafts that can't be shortened, and usually improved in the process.

Think About Consequences   The worst thing that can happen is that a Sun sales pro is in a meeting with a hot prospect, and someone on the customer's side pulls out a print-out of your blog and says "This person at Sun says that product sucks."

In general, "XXX sucks" is not only risky but unsubtle. Saying "Netbeans needs to have an easier learning curve for the first-time user" is fine; saying "Visual Development Environments for Java sucks" is just amateurish.

Once again, it's all about judgment: using your weblog to trash or embarrass the company, our customers, or your co-workers, is not only dangerous but stupid.

Disclaimers   Many bloggers put a disclaimer on their front page saying who they work for, but that they're not speaking officially. This is good practice, but don't count on it to avoid trouble; it may not have much legal effect.

Tools   We're starting to develop tools to make it easy for anyone to start publishing, but if you feel the urge, don't wait for us; there are lots of decent blogging tools and hosts out there.

Sample Blogging Policy and
Code of Ethics by Forrester's Charlene Li

Charlene Li is a principal analyst for Forrester who specializes in technology and how it impacts media and marketing. She's a respected blogger in her own right at http://forrester.typepad.com/charleneli. She separates a blogging policy, with caveats on respecting confidentiality and proprietary information, from "how to blog," which she calls a code of ethics.

Sample Corporate Blogging Policy

1. Make it clear that the views expressed in the blog are yours alone and do not necessarily represent the views of your employer.
2. Respect the company's confidentiality and proprietary information.
3. Ask your manager if you have any questions about what is appropriate to include in your blog.
4. Be respectful to the company, employees, customers, partners, and competitors.
5. Understand when the company asks that topics not be discussed for confidentiality or legal compliance reasons.
6. Ensure that your blogging activity does not interfere with your work commitments.

Sample Blogger Code of Ethics

1. I will tell the truth.
2. I will write deliberately and with accuracy.
3. I will acknowledge and correct mistakes promptly.
4. I will preserve the original post, using notations to show where I have made changes so as to maintain the integrity of my publishing.

5. I will never delete a post.
6. I will not delete comments unless they are spam or off-topic.
7. I will reply to emails and comments when appropriate, and do so promptly.
8. I will strive for high quality with every post—including basic spellchecking.
9. I will stay on topic.
10. I will disagree with other opinions respectfully.
11. I will link to online references and original source materials directly.
12. I will disclose conflicts of interest.
13. I will keep private issues and topics private, since discussing private issues would jeopardize my personal and work relationships.

Thomas Nelson Blogging Guidelines

Thomas Nelson developed its guidelines through an iterative process that included input from the company's lawyers as well as readers of CEO Mike Hyatt's blog (where an earlier version was first published). The guidelines make it clear what the business reason is for encouraging employees to blog: to open the door and offer a peek inside one of the world's largest publishers. And to update the 200-year-old publishing company's image. Note the tie-in to The Company Handbook as the last point.

At Thomas Nelson, we want to encourage you to blog about our company, our products, and your work. Our goal is three-fold:

- To raise the visibility of our company,

- To make a contribution to our industry, and

- To give the public a look at what goes on within a real live publishing company.

Therefore, we have established a "blog aggregator page" that is linked to the ThomasNelson.com Web site. "House Work," the name of this page, contains links to employee blogs, along with the first few sentences from the most recent entry. The page is automatically updated whenever a blogger creates a new post. This way readers can quickly scan new entries, click on those that interest them, and then read the entry on the blogger's site. This makes it convenient for people who are interested in reading employee blogs. It also helps publicize individual blogs and generates traffic for everyone.

In order to give some direction to employees who wish to blog, we have established a "Blog Oversight Committee" or "BOC." This is a group of fellow-employee bloggers who are committed to promoting blogging within our company and making sure that the Company's interests are served.

If you would like to have us link to your blog, you must submit it to the BOC. Before doing so, you should design your blog and write at least one entry. Once you have done this, send an e-mail to [name] with a link to your blog. The BOC will then review your blog and notify you whether or not it meets the criteria.

In order to participate in this program, you must abide by the following guidelines. (Please keep in mind that review by the BOC and participation in this program does not absolve you of responsibility for everything you post.)

1. **Start with a blogging service.** We do not host employee blogs. We think it adds more credibility if the Company does not officially sponsor them. Therefore, please use one of the many third-party blog hosting sites on the Internet. Some of these are free, such as Blogger.com, LiveJournal.com, Blog-City.com, Xanga.com, and MSN Spaces. Others charge a nominal fee. Examples include TypePad.com, SquareSpace.com, BlogIdentity.com, and Bubbler.com. If you use one of the latter, any expense is your responsibility.

2. **Write as yourself.** In other words, please use your real name. We don't want people writing anonymously or under a pseudonym. Your name should be prominently displayed on your blog's title or subtitle. This will add credibility with your readers and promote accountability within our company.

3. **Own your content.** Employee blog sites are not Company communications. Therefore, your blog entries legally belong to you. They represent your thoughts and opinions. We think it is important that you remind your readers of this fact by including the following disclaimer on your site: "The posts on this blog are provided 'as is' with no warranties and confer no rights. The opinions expressed on this site are my own and do

not necessarily represent those of my employer." You assume full responsibility and liability for all actions arising from your posts. We also encourage you to put a copyright notice on your site in your name (e.g., "© 2005, John Smith").

4. **Write relevant.** Write often. Whether you know it or not, you are an expert. You have a unique perspective on our company based on your talents, skills, and current responsibilities. People what to hear about that perspective. Also, in order to develop a consistent readership, you should try to write on a regular basis. For some, this will be daily; for others, it may be weekly. The important thing is consistent posting. New content is what keeps readers coming back. You may also write on company time, provided it doesn't become excessive and doesn't interfere with your job assignments and responsibilities.

5. **Advertise—if you wish.** While there is no requirement to run ads on your blog, you are free to do this if you wish. Some of the free blog services run ads as a way to offset their costs. If you use such a service, you won't have a choice. On the other hand, if you pay for your service, you can avoid advertising altogether or participate in a service like Google's AdSense or Amazon's Associate Program. These types of programs will pay you based on "page views," "click-throughs," or purchases made on participating Web sites. You might want to ask the BOC or fellow bloggers for suggestions. The only thing we ask is that, to the extent you have control, you run ads or recommend products that are congruent with our core values as a Company.

6. **Be nice.** Avoid attacking other individuals or companies. This includes fellow employees, authors, customers, vendors, competitors, or shareholders. You are welcome to disagree with the Company's leaders, provided your tone is respectful. If in doubt, we suggest that you "sleep on it" and then submit your entry to the BOC before posting it on your blog.

7. **Keep secrets.** Do not disclose sensitive, proprietary, confidential, or financial information about the Company, other than what is publicly available in our SEC filings and corporate press releases. This includes revenues, profits, forecasts, and other financial information related to specific authors, brands, products, product lines, customers, operating units, etc. Again, if in doubt, check with the BOC before posting this type of information.

8. **Respect copyrights.** For your protection, do not post any material that is copyrighted unless (a) you are the copyright owner, (b) you have written permission of the copyright owner to post the copyrighted material on your blog, or (c) you are sure that the use of any copyrighted material is permitted by the legal doctrine of "fair use." (Please note: this is your responsibility. The Company cannot provide you with legal advice regarding this.)

9. **Obey the law.** This goes without saying, but by way of reminder, do not post any material that is obscene, defamatory, profane, libelous, threatening, harassing, abusive, hateful, embarrassing to another person or entity, or violates the privacy rights of another. Also, do not post material that contains viruses, Trojan horses, worms, or any other computer code that is intended to damage, interfere with, or surreptitiously intercept or expropriate any system, data, or information.

10. **Remember the handbook.** As a condition of your employment, you agreed to abide by the rules of the Thomas Nelson Company Handbook. This also applies to your blogging activities. We suggest you take time to review the section entitled, "Employee Responsibilities" (pp. 36–39).

If you do not abide by the above guidelines, we reserve the right to stop linking to your blog.

Examples of Disclaimers on Employee Blogs

It's considered a best practice to include a disclaimer on an employee blog. Typically the disclaimer states that the blogger's words do not represent the views of the company. Implicit is the fact that the blog has not been vetted by the corporate comunications department. A disclaimer also tacitly acknowledges that the blogger is employed by an organization that allows—or encourages—blogging.

Safe Harbor Disclaimer on a Company Officer's Blog

Dave Hitz is founder and executive vice president of Network Appliance. NetApp, as it's called, is a global technology company that provides data backup and recovery. Dave's blog is prominently featured with a Quick Link on NetApp's home page. The Safe Harbor Disclaimer below can be find through a link at the bottom of his blog page at blogs.netapp.com/dave. The disclaimer means that Dave won't get in hot water with the SEC for something he writes on his blog—as long as it's information that would ordinarily be included in the company's official filings with the regulatory agency. Put another way, he's not going to reveal any company secrets.

Author's blog may contain forward-looking statements that involve risks and uncertainties. Forward-looking statements include any statement regarding future events or the future financial performance of *Company Name* that involves risks or uncertainties. In evaluating these statements, readers should specifically consider various factors that could cause actual events or results to differ materially from those indicated, including without limitation: continuing decline in the general economic conditions, customer demand for products and services, customer acceptance of product architectures, increased competition, and other important factors as described in *Company Name* reports and documents filed from time to time with the Securities and Exchange Commission, including its mostly recently submitted 10-K and 10-Q.

"Safe Harbor" Statement under U.S. Private Securities Litigation Reform Act of 1995.

Microsoft employee Kevin Briody included the following tongue-in-cheek but pointed disclaimer on an earlier version of his blog at www.seattleduck.com.

Example of Employee Disclaimer

As the lawyers make us say:

The posts on this blog are provided "as is" with no warranties, and confer no rights. The opinions expressed herein are my own and do not represent my employer's views in any way. Nothing posted here should be considered official or sanctioned by my employer or any other organization I'm affiliated with.

In English:

Although I work for Microsoft, nothing I say here is endorsed or reviewed by the company prior to posting. Just my own ramblings. If you take issue with any comments, they are with me alone.

Do Not Blog This

Another convention that's taking hold is the practice of including a "Do not blog this" notice at the end of an email message. Author and blogger Seth Godin's version says: "This note is intended as an informal communication and is off the record for blogs and other publications, unless we agree otherwise." In other words, not everything is bloggable—unless you ask first. A good reminder that after you hit Publish, you've created a permanent, public Web page for all the world to read. And that not everyone's musings, opinions and off-the-cuff remarks are fodder for a blog.

LEGAL RESOURCES

Consult your own legal counsel, of course. But the following resources offer a good introduction to the range of legal issues associated with blogging—from copyright and freedom of speech to employee rights and reporter's privilege (the protections extended to journalists).

Electronic Frontier Foundation's Legal Guide for Bloggers

EFF's comprehensive and readable guide is available free at www.eff.org/bloggers/lg/. It includes FAQs on intellectual property, online defamation and workplace blogging, along with a helpful section on Section 230 of the Communication Decency Act of 1996. Basically, this law protects Web hosting services, including blogs, from liability for the content of material *created by third parties* and published on their sites. In plain language, generally you can't be sued for what's written in comments posted to your blog. Very little case law exists in this area as yet.

Media Law Resource Center

You will find a list of libel and related lawsuits against bloggers at medialaw.org.

NewPRWiki's Resources for Legal Problems and Blogs

This useful list of links is continually updated by volunteer editors at thenewpr.com/wiki/pmwiki.php?pagename=Resources. LegalProblems.

BLOG DESIGN AND USABILITY

Jakob Nielsen, principal of the Nielsen Norman Group, is one of the first and most respected Web usability gurus. He has published his online Alertbox column since 1995. This article from October 2005 is a must-read based on common sense and sound Web design principles. You can browse the Alertbox archives at useit.com/alertbox. This column is online at useit.com/alertbox/weblogs.html. Reprinted with permission.

Weblog Usability: The Top Ten Design Mistakes

By Jakob Nielsen

Summary: Weblogs are often too internally focused and ignore key usability issues, making it hard for new readers to understand the site and trust the author.

Weblogs are a form of website. The thousands of normal website usability guidelines therefore apply to them . . . But weblogs are also a special genre of website; they have unique characteristics and thus distinct usability problems.

One of a weblog's great benefits is that it essentially frees you from "Web design." You write a paragraph, click a button, and it's posted on the Internet. No need for visual design, page design, interaction design, information architecture, or any programming or server maintenance.

Weblogs make having a simple website much easier, and as a result, the number of people who write for the Web has exploded. This is a striking confirmation of the importance of ease of use.

Weblogs' second benefit is that they're a Web-native content genre: they rely on links, and short postings prevail. You don't have to write a full article or conduct original research or reporting. You can simply find something interesting on another site and link to it, possibly with commentary or additional examples. Obviously, this is much easier than running a conventional site, and again indicates the benefits of lowering the barriers to computer use.

As a third benefit, weblogs are part of an ecosystem (often called the Blogosphere) that serves as a positive feedback loop: Whatever good postings exist are promoted through links from other sites. More reader/writers see this good stuff, and the very best then get linked to even more. As a result, link frequency follows a Zipf distribution, with disproportionally more links to the best postings.

Some weblogs are really just private diaries intended only for a handful of family members and close friends. Usability guidelines generally don't apply to such sites, because the readers' prior knowledge and motivation are incomparably greater than those of third-party users. When you want to reach new readers who aren't your mother, however, usability becomes important.

Also, while readers of your intranet weblog might know you, usability is important because your readers are on company time.

Usability Issues

To reach new readers and respect your existing readers' time constraints, test your weblog against the following usability problems.

1. No Author Biographies
Unless you're a business blog, you probably don't need a full-fledged "about us" section the way a corporate site does. That said, the basic rationale for "about us" translates directly into the need for an "about me" page on a weblog: users want to know who they're dealing with.

It's a simple matter of trust. Anonymous writings have less credence than something that's signed. And, unless a person's extraordinarily famous, it's not enough to simply say that Joe Blogger writes the content. Readers want to know more about Joe. Does he have any credentials or experience in the field he's commenting on? (Even if you don't have formal credentials, readers will trust you more if you're honest about that fact, set forth your informal experience, and explain the reason for your enthusiasm.)

2. No Author Photo

Even weblogs that provide author bios often omit the author photo. A photo is important for two reasons:

- It offers a more personable impression of the author. You enhance your credibility by the simple fact that you're not trying to hide. Also, users relate more easily to somebody they've seen.

- It connects the virtual and physical worlds. People who've met you before will recognize your photo, and people who've read your site will recognize you when you meet in person (say, at a conference—or the company cafeteria if you're an intranet blogger).

A huge percentage of the human brain is dedicated to remembering and recognizing faces. For many, faces work better than names. I learned this lesson myself in 1987 when I included my photo in a HyperCard stack I authored that was widely disseminated on Mac-oriented BBSs. Over the next two years, countless people came up to me and said, "I liked your stack," having recognized me from the photo.

Also, if you run a professional weblog and expect to be quoted in the press, you should follow the recommendations for using the Web for PR and include a selection of high-resolution photos that photo editors can download.

3. Nondescript Posting Titles

Sadly, even though weblogs are native to the Web, authors rarely follow the guidelines for writing for the Web in terms of making content scannable. This applies to a posting's body text, but it's even more important with headlines. Users must be able to grasp the gist of an article by reading its headline. Avoid cute or humorous headlines that make no sense out of context.

Your posting's title is microcontent and you should treat it as a writing project in its own right. On a value-per-word basis, headline writing is the most important writing you do.

Descriptive headlines are especially important for representing your weblog in search engines, newsfeeds (RSS), and other external environments. In those contexts, users often see only the headline and use it to determine whether to click into the full posting. Even if users see a short abstract along with the headline (as with most search engines), user testing shows that people often read only the headline. In fact, people often read only the first three or four words of a headline when scanning a list of possible places to go. Sample bad headlines:

- What Is It That You Want?

- Hey, kids! Comics!

- Victims Abandoned

Sample good headlines:

- Pictures from Die Hunns and Black Halos show

- Office Depot Pays United States $4.75 Million to Resolve False Claims Act Allegations (too long, but even if you only read the first few words, you have an idea of what it's about)

- Ice cream trucks as church marketing

This last headline works on a church-related blog. If you're writing an ice cream industry blog, start the headline with the word "church" because it's the information-carrying word within a context of all ice cream, all the time.

In browsing weblog headline listings to extract these examples, I noticed several headlines in ALL CAPS. That's always bad. Reading speed is reduced by 10% and users are put off by the appearance of shouting.

4. Links Don't Say Where They Go
Many weblog authors seem to think it's cool to write link anchors like: "some people think" or "there's more here and here." Remember one of the basics of the Web: Life is too short to click on an unknown. Tell people where they're going and what they'll find at the other end of the link.

Generally, you should provide predictive information in either the anchor text itself or the immediately surrounding words. You can also use link titles for supplementary information that doesn't fit with your content.

A related mistake in this category is to use insider shorthand, such as using first names when you reference other writers or weblogs. Unless you're writing only for your friends, don't alienate new visitors by appearing to be part of a closed clique. The Web is not high school.

5. Classic Hits Are Buried
Hopefully, you'll write some pieces with lasting value for readers outside your fan base. Don't relegate such classics to the archives, where people can only find something if they know you posted it, say, in May 2003.

Highlight a few evergreens in your navigation system and link directly to them. For example, my own list of almost 300 Alertbox columns starts by saying, "Read these first: Usability 101 and Top Ten Mistakes of Web Design."

Also, remember to link to your past pieces in newer postings. Don't assume that readers have been with you from the beginning; give them background and context in case they want to read more about your ideas.

6. The Calendar Is the Only Navigation

A timeline is rarely the best information architecture, yet it's the default way to navigate weblogs. Most weblog software provides a way to categorize postings so users can easily get a list of all postings on a certain topic. Do use categorization, but avoid the common mistake of tagging a posting with almost all of your categories. Be selective. Decide on a few places where a posting most belongs.

Categories must be sufficiently detailed to lead users to a thoroughly winnowed list of postings. At the same time, they shouldn't be so detailed that users face a category menu that's overly long and difficult to scan. Ten to twenty categories are appropriate for structuring many topics.

On the main page for each category, highlight that category's evergreens as well as a timeline of its most recent postings.

7. Irregular Publishing Frequency

Establishing and meeting user expectations is one of the fundamental principles of Web usability. For a weblog, users must be able to anticipate when and how often updates will occur.

For most weblogs, daily updates are probably best, but weekly or even monthly updates might work as well, depending on your topic. In either case, pick a publication schedule and stick to it. If you usually post daily but sometimes let months go by without new content, you'll lose many of your loyal—and thus most valuable—readers.

Certainly, you shouldn't post when you have nothing to say. Polluting cyberspace with excess information is a sin. To ensure regular publishing, hold back some ideas and post them when you hit a dry spell.

8. Mixing Topics

If you publish on many different topics, you're less likely to attract a loyal audience of high-value users. Busy people might visit a blog to read an entry about a topic that interests them. They're unlikely to return, however, if their target topic appears only sporadically among a massive range of postings on other topics. The only people who read everything are those with too much time on their hands (a low-value demographic).

The more focused your content, the more focused your readers. That, again, makes you more influential within your niche. Specialized sites rule the Web, so aim tightly.

If you have the urge to speak out on, say, both American foreign policy and the business strategy of Internet telephony, establish two blogs. You can always interlink them when appropriate.

9. Forgetting That You Write for Your Future Boss

Whenever you post anything to the Internet—whether on a weblog, in a discussion group, or even in an email—think about how it will look to a hiring manager in ten years. Once stuff's out, it's archived, cached, and indexed in many services that you might never be aware of.

Years from now, someone might consider hiring you for a plum job and take the precaution of 'nooping (checking you out online) first. (Just taking a stab at what's next after Google. Rest assured: there will be some super-snooper service that'll dredge up anything about you that's ever been bitified.) What will they find in terms of naïvely puerile "analysis" or offendingly nasty flames published under your name?

Think twice before posting. If you don't want your future boss to read it, don't post.

10. Having a Domain Name Owned by a Weblog Service

Having a weblog address ending in blogspot.com, typepad.com, etc. will soon be the equivalent of having an @aol.com email address or a Geocities website: the mark of a naïve beginner who shouldn't be taken too seriously.

Letting somebody else own your name means that they own your destiny on the Internet. They can degrade the service quality as much as they want. They can increase the price as much as they want. They can add atop your content as many pop-ups, blinking banners, or other user-repelling advertising techniques as they want. They can promote your competitor's offers on your pages. Yes, you can walk, but at the cost of your loyal readers, links you've attracted from other sites, and your search engine ranking.

The longer you stay at someone else's domain name, the higher the cost of going independent. Yes, it's tempting to start a new weblog on one of the services that offer free accounts. It's easy, it's quick, and it's obviously cheap. But it only costs $8 per year to get your personal domain name and own your own future. As soon as you realize you're serious about blogging, move it away from a domain name that's controlled by somebody else. The longer you delay, the more pain you'll feel when you finally make the move.

Top Five Design Features to Build Into Your Blog

by Rok Hrastnik of MarketingStudies.net

[Rok Hrastnik is an expert on RSS and marketing. Based in Slovenia, he is e-commerce manager for Studio Moderna, the leading direct marketing agency for Central and Eastern Europe. He maintains several information rich blogs on the topic of RSS as a marketing tool at MarketingStudies.net. His tips on attracting email subscribers to a blog—while at the same time educating your readers on how to subscribe via RSS—are spot on. Note the importance of providing an interim RSS information page. You can use FeedBurner.com (it's free) to create such a page for your blog.]

Many serious bloggers sneer at using email as a way to notify readers of new entries. They prefer to send a ping via RSS. As a business blogger you can't afford to make this mistake. Most people either don't use RSS or don't know what it is. Provide your blog readers with an option to subscribe to a weekly "best blog posts" email ezine and perhaps even a daily blog email update.

1. Take a Proactive Approach to Signing Up Email Subscribers to Your Blog

The place for an email subscription box is not somewhere down on the right, but directly below your header in the *left-hand column.* Use benefit-driven copy to prompt your visitors to take notice of the subscription option. "Subscribe to our blog posts" won't cut it. Try something like, "Too busy to visit this blog everyday? Like what you're reading? Subscribe to our email update and you won't miss a thing."

2. No Left-hand Column?

Your blog doesn't have a left-hand column? Um, where is your navigation? Remember, there's absolutely no such thing as right-hand navigation. People are used to using links in the left-hand column to find their way around a Web site and you're not going to change that.

3. Really Start Generating RSS Subscribers

Having an RSS feed subscribe button somewhere on the bottom of your blog template won't work. Either put the button in your header or in your left-hand column directly below the email subscription box. Entice people to subscribe. For those who have no idea what RSS is, provide a link to an RSS information page. Then include links to subscribe via RSS from that page. Also include direct subscription buttons for My Yahoo!, Google, NewsGator, Bloglines and other popular RSS newsreaders.

4. Top Content—Your Best Blog Entries

If you update your blog frequently, your less recent content keeps being pushed down the page, where most of your blog readers will never bother to look for it. Overcome this functional feature of blogs by creating a list of your top posts, clearly displayed on every blog page. Depending on the topic you cover, you might want to place these headlines as close to the top of your blog as possible, in order to quickly entice your new visitors to start reading the best of what you have to offer.

5. Lead Your Visitors to Your MDA (Most Desired Action)

Use your blog to lead people to the action you most want them to take on your corporate site. For example, subscribing to your ezine, requesting more information or ordering a product. Experiment by incorporating the copy for your MDA at the bottom of each blog post (this requires a technical tweak) as well as displaying it prominently in your side columns. And if you're providing multiple services or products, promote each of them next to the appropriate posts, based on post topics. (Again, this can be done using blog software like MovableType and WordPress.)

Recommended Reading

Blogwild!, by Andy Wibbels
Lively step-by-step guide that shows you how to set up a blog using TypePad.

Buzz Marketing with Blogs for Dummies, by Susannah Gardner
Practical, well-illustrated guide. Excellent overview of the basics of business blogging. Includes numerous examples as well as snapshots of blogging history.

The Elements of Style Illustrated, by William Strunk Jr., E.B. White, Maira Kalman
It's OK to be a bit breezier than they suggest. Otherwise, this classic guide to clear writing is essential reading for good blogging. The new edition with Kalman's additions is marvelous.

The Big Moo, by the Group of 33 and edited by Seth Godin
A series of provocative essays that will prompt you to think differently about marketing and doing business, period. Builds on Godin's theme of being "remarkable."

Cashing in with Content, by David Meerman Scott
Profiles of 20 Web marketers who use content to turn browsers into buyers. Included are the *Wall Street Journal*, UPS, Alcoa, Dean for America and Booz Allen Hamilton.

The Cluetrain Manifesto, by Rick Levine, Christopher Locke, Doc Searls and David Weinberger
The classic tome that posits the now accepted wisdom: markets are conversations. A precursor, of course, to the blogging phenomenon.

Naked Conversations: How Blogs Are Changing the Way Businesses Talk with Customers, by Robert Scoble and Shel Israel
An anecdote-rich history of business blogging by Microsoft's chief blogger, Robert Scoble, and his co-author, Shel Israel. Another one for your blogging bookshelf.

The Search: How Google and Its Rivals Rewrote the Rules of Business and Transformed Our Culture, by John Battelle
The inside story of how Google's business model evolved. A reminder of the importance of being "found" by Google and why you want your blog to appear at the top of search results.

The Weblog Handbook, by Rebecca Blood
The original book about blogging, elegantly written and with a focus on how to write.

A Whole New Mind: Moving from the Information Age to the Conceptual Age, by Daniel H. Pink
Good blogging—passionate, authentic—is as much a right-brain activity as it is a left.

The World Is Flat: A Brief History of the Twenty-First Century, by Thomas L. Friedman
This guy really gets it. Detailed explanation of the global supply chain and how it flattens the world economy. Blogging is part of the information supply chain for individuals.

ANATOMY OF A BLOG

Posted by Debbie Weil on May 04, 2005 at 11:12 PM in <u>Blogging 101,</u>
<u>Corporate Blogging Guidelines, E-newsletters vs blogs, Etiquette,</u>
<u>Writing Tips</u> | <u>Permalink</u> | <u>Comments (0)</u> | <u>Trackback (1)</u>

So what will it take for the Fortune 500 to adopt blogging?

David Kline, co-author of one of the handful of books
published thus far on blogging (Blog! <u>How the Newest Media</u>
<u>Revolution Is Changing Politics, Business, and Culture</u>) just
emailed to say he's working on an article about what's holding
the F500 back from blogging and what it will take for blogging

---

BASIC FEATURES

1. **Author:** identifies who wrote a particular entry. Especially useful on group blogs.
2. **Date and time:** indicates when blog entry was posted.
3. **Categories:** entries are grouped into sets, which show at a glance the topic of the post.
4. **Comments:** readers can interact with the author and other readers by leaving a relevant comment.
5. **TrackBack:** a way to track conversations that are continued on other blogs.
6. **Title:** uses specific keyword phrases in order to get found in search engine results.
7. **Body of entry:** includes lots of links to other blogs or online resources.

BlogWrite for CEOs

Debbie Weil on CEO blogs, writing a thought leadership blog and the corporate blogging phenomenon.

« Update on IABC blogging panel | Main | Why more CEOs aren't blogging (yet), according to USA Today »

Blogging 101 Resources

Been collecting these for a week or so.

- Ran across this nifty page on Robert's Echo blog. Includes everything from the "origin" of blogs, stats on blog readership, recommended PR blogs, link to a Forrester Research executive summary, lists of internal and external corporate blogs and more.

- Another page with all things blog (including links to RSS tutorials and basic blog definitions) penned by the Singapore-based Rambling Librarian.

- Comprehensive list from Dave Taylor's Intuitive Life blog with links to other articles.

- 101 writing tips from Karl Chisholm on writing a thought leadership blog. (He writes a grassroots advocacy blog.)

Posted by Debbie Weil on May 04, 2005 at 11:12 PM in **Blogging 101,** **Corporate Blogging Guidelines, E-newsletters vs blogs, Etiquette, Writing Tips | Permalink | Comments (0) | Trackback (1)**

So what will it take for the Fortune 500 to adopt blogging?

David Kline, co-author of one of the handful of books published thus far on blogging (Blog! How the Newest Media Revolution Is Changing Politics, Business, and Culture) just emailed to say he's working on an article about what's holding the F500 back from blogging and what it will take for blogging

(1) ABOUT

SEARCH THIS SITE

(2) Google™ [____] Go

ADDING A COMMENT TO THIS BLOG (3)

Because I value your thoughtful opinions, I encourage you to add a comment to any entry on this blog.

USEFUL LINKS

(4) 🔳

CONTACT

(5) Debbie Weil WordBiz.com, Inc. 3601 Newark St. NW Washington, DC 20016 +1 202.364.5705

(6) wordbiz @ GMail.com

ALSO VISIT...

Book blog for "The Corporate Blogging Book: Absolutely Everything You Need to Know to Get it Right" (Penguin Portfolio 2006)

She's back! MonaLisaOfBlogging

Consulting, in-house training & speaking on how to launch a corporate blog

CEO BLOGS (7)

Alan Meckler · Jupiter Media

Bill Nussey · Silverpop

Bob Kramer · LiveVault

Bob Lutz · GM

Bob Parsons · Go Daddy

Bob Sutor · IBM

Brian Carroll · B2B Lead Generation

Bud Bilanich · OEG Consulting

Buzz Bruggeman · Active Words

Chris Baggott · ExactTarget

Chris Mercer · Mercer Capital

Dan Lynn · Digital Grit

ADDITIONAL FEATURES

1. **About link:** a useful shortcut to learn more about the author and the focus of the blog.
2. **Search box:** enables you to search the contents of the blog.
3. **Comment disclaimer:** not yet in widespread use but youll see it more frequently as blog authors clarify their policies.
4. **RSS button:** universally recognized icon that indicates your blog's RSS feed. Best if it links to an interim page explaining how to subscribe via RSS. You can also include a subscribe via email box.
5. **Contact:** essential contact information should be clearly visible.
6. **Links back to the main site:** a blog can drive traffic back to important pages on a company's main Web site.
7. **Recommended resources:** readers like to find more information related to the topic of your blog.

Get Smart Glossary

adverblog   A blog created for the purpose of promoting a product, brand or service. May have a limited life span. One of the first was Nike's Art of Speed at gawker.com/artofspeed. Some *character blogs* are adverblogs. Using a blog in this way is also known as blogvertising.

AJAX   Stands for Asynchronous Javascript and XML. Sounds techie but it's cool. A way to create real-time Web applications. Examples are Writely.com, a Web-based, collaborative writing tool and Kiko, an interactive online calendar.

archives   When entries become old news, they don't die. Instead they retire to the electronic rocking chair, waiting for the occasional chance to tell their story again.

blog   Contraction of Web and log.

blog carnival   A long blog entry that showcases a specific topic by linking to other blog posts on that issue and adding editorial commentary. In other words, deliberately builds on clever stuff other folks have written. Longest running carnival is Carnival of the Vanities. It moves around to different blogs as different hosts take turns publishing it.

blog client   Software or application for blogging. A blog client is at your service and awaits your next post to share with the world. Also known as blog software and blogware.

blog evangelizing   When you're the one waving the flag inside your company and trying to persuade others that blogs are more useful than cool.

blogger relations   The blog version of public relations. The art of successfully engaging with the blogosphere to monitor, participate or advertise on blogs. Increasingly, companies or non-profts seek out influential bloggers to encourage them to blog about their products, services or advocacy campaigns. Sometimes a financial or other incentive is offered (hey, try out our newest cell phone) although this practice is frowned upon by blogging purists. See bloggerrelations.com.

bloggerati   A-List bloggers as determined by number of visitors to their blogs as well as influence and credibility. These are the "cool" people in the sometimes junior high world of blogging.

bloggerheads   A take-off on "at loggerheads." Groups or individual bloggers who are in heated disagreement with one another.

blogiverse   A combination of blog and universe. See *blogosphere.*

blogosphere   The collective community of blogs. Unlike the Borg collective, assimilation is frowned upon. Bloggers have a mind of their own. Sometimes referred to as blogistan or *blogiverse.*

blogviator   I made this one up. Think bloviator.

blog oversight committee   Refers to a committee in a corporate environment that works to promote and manage blogging within the company. (Ref: *1984,* by George Orwell, the book that introduced the idea of "big brother watching you."). Also known as BOC.

blogroll   List of a blogger's favorite blogs. Often the blogger's buddies or people the blogger is brown nosing in hopes will they add his or her blog to their lists.

blog swarm   When the blogosphere experiences a large amount of activity, postings, commentary and opinions on a topic or controversy. No insect repellant required. Also known as blogstorm.

blogvertising   See *adverblogging.*

blogware   See *blog client.*

blogworking   Content-rich sites with blog communities or group blogs enabling members to network with other professionals. Examples are adholes.com (for the ad industry) and alwayson-network.com (for the technology, media and entertainment industry).

blogophobic   What it sounds like. Companies large and small can suffer from this condition.

blook   A book whose contents came verbatim—or in concept—from a blog. Conversely, a blook is also a blog that publishes a book in installments (much as Charles Dickens's novels were published in serial form in the 19th century).

categories   The secret of blogging as a low-cost but highly effective content management system (CMS). Assign a category—or several—to every entry you post to your blog. For example, "conferences," "free downloads," "industry metrics," "top tips." Soon you'll have a rich repository that is searchable by topic as well as date.

CBO   Chief Blogging Officer. Began as a tongue-in-cheek takeoff on the many CXX or chief yadda yadda officer titles. The CBO can be a blog editor or a senior-level executive. Duties include blog evangelizing within and outside the company as well as managing the corporate blog. This title may catch on as more corporations adopt blogging programs.

CGM   See *consumer-generated media*.

character blogs   Beware! These are branding blogs sponsored by a company and "written" by a fictitious cartoon or literary character. Frowned upon by purists as fake because they mock the authenticity of blogging. However, anything goes in blogdom. A character blog can be clever and effective, like T. Alexander, the epicurean guide to gourmet food e-tailer GourmetStation at gourmetstationblog.typepad.com.

chat room   An online forum where multiple users chat (type) to each other in a live, real-time conversation. Be prepared when entering: a chat room has its own language with conventions such as BTW (by the way), FWIW (for what it's worth), gr8 (great) and GTG (got to go).

consumer-generated media   A new concept in marketing, often referred to as CGM. It means any form of content created and posted online by consumers. Includes message boards, blog entries, comments left on blogs, podcasting, viral videos, reviews on sites like Amazon and Epinions and more. Studies show consumers are more influenced by CGM than traditional advertising when making a purchase decision.

citizen journalists   Bloggers who publish breaking news stories as well as report on and analyze the news of the day, thus co-opting or complementing the work of mainstream journalists.

comments   A permanent part of a blog's content that is added by readers of the blog. Typically, you click on a Comments link at the end of a blog entry and type in your comment. They give readers the opportunity to question, discuss, adulate or flame the blogger's entry.

comment spam   Comments left on blog entries by spammers. They have nothing to do with the topic of the blog and often include links to drug, gambling, pornographic and other "not safe for viewing at work or home" sites. You can set up your Comments for delayed approval so that these don't get published.

corporate blog   A blog officially published by a company with the purpose of helping the organization reach specific goals. An engaging corporate blog puts a human face on a company and gives it an individual, distinctive voice.

corposphere   the business blogosphere.

creative commons license   Gives bloggers, writers, artists and musicians a way to deliberately forego some copyright protection by granting permission to reprint or repost their material, with attribution—for *non-commercial* use—including audio, images, video, and text. Why? So you get your stuff out there, circulating around and subtly promoting your expertise or talents. See creativecommons.org.

dead wood media   Mainstream print media that relies on the, er, destruction of forests to print the paper version of their content. Also known as dead tree media, dead tree edition, and old media.

dooced To get fired for a post written in a blog or on a Web site that the blogger's employer finds objectionable. Word comes from Heather Armstrong's blog, Dooce.com, which is consistently in the Technorati Top 100. She was fired from a Los Angeles software firm after venting in her blog about her company. Prompted a blogswarm around the issue of employee blogging and blogophobic bosses.

entry The meaty part of a blog, i.e., the individual articles or short posts written by the blogger. Also known as a post.

entry title Catchy and keyword-friendly header for a blog entry. An effective title will grab readers' attention and is more apt to be found by the search engines.

external blog Public blog that is open for anyone to read and for the search engines to find. Not a good place to vent about your boss.

fake blogs Blogs disguised to look and read like a blog when they're nothing but pages with links or links to affiliated Web sites to rake in revenue. These blogs depend on ads related to the blog's content and often steal content from legitimate blogs as a way to generate commissions through Google's AdSense or other ad programs. Aka splogs or spam blogs.

FAQ Frequently Asked Question. An FAQ is a typical feature on business Web sites. Ostensibly, it's a Web page or pages with questions and answers about the company's products or services. The FAQ pages are often artificially constructed with the Web editor asking questions that prompt answers the company wants you to hear.

flame Both noun and verb. When a person writes a derogatory, hot-blooded, or juvenile comment on another blog, he or she is flaming. Can appear in comments on blogs, forums, and email discussion lists.

folksonomy A combination of "folks" and "taxonomy" to mean, literally, "people's classification management." Mostly a fancy word for *tagging.* Sites like del.icio.us and Flickr are based on folksonomy. In other words, users assign their own categories or tags to each piece of content, whether it's a written blog post, an audio file or a photo. Over time, consistent tags emerge as a result of this collaborative effort.

forum   Online discussion sites where members typically post messages, often questions and answers, on specific topics. Unlike a blog, which has a single owner or publisher, anyone can publish content to a forum. Also known as bulletin board, discussion board or message board.

Google bomb   When a large number of bloggers attempt to influence Google's rankings for a word or phrase by linking it to an unrelated Web page. The most famous example is the phrase "miserable failure." Type it into Google. The result? George W. Bush appears first in the search results.

grok   Slang word that means to fully understand something. Word was first used in *Stranger in a Strange Land*, by Robert A. Heinlein, where it meant (in Martian), "to drink." After reading this book, do you grok blogs?

group blog   A blog with more than one contributing publisher or writer. A good example is PR firm Hill & Knowlton's Collective Conversation at blogs.hillandknowlton.com.

hack   Contrary to the negative reputation of the verb (hacking), a hack (noun) is considered a clever way to enhance the functionality of a Web site or online software. As an example, see Steve Rubel's Ten Blogging Hacks at Micropersuasion.com/2005/11/ten_blogging_ha.html.

hits   What most bloggers want lots of and what they look for in their blog statistics. In other words, traffic. A hit doesn't necessarily represent a unique visitor, however. When the same visitor reloads a Web site multiple times, it creates multiple hits.

host   The computer or server where a Web site's files physically live and are accessed. Web sites for large companies normally reside on internal servers. Small businesses and individuals typically pay a monthly fee for external Web or blog hosting services.

internal blog Blogs on an intranet that only those behind a company's firewall can access. They are useful for team collaboration and knowledge management as well as personal commentary. Sometimes called a dark blog.

k-log meaning knowledge log. Internal blogs used for sharing project or company information. Also known as Klog and K-blog.

joblogging Blogging as a way to attract the eyes of a recruiter or potential employer. Human resources departments increasingly search for and read applicants' blogs as part of the vetting process. A well-written blog reveals whether a candidate can think and write clearly—a rare talent these days.

mashup A Web-based application that combines information or functionality from one or more sites to create something new. For example, HousingMaps (housingmaps.com) combines Google Maps (maps.google.com) with Craig's List (craigslist.org) to map out homes or rooms for sale or for rent. Also spelled with a hyphen— mash-up.

meme Überblogger Doc Searls, one of the co-authors of *The Cluetrain Manifeso*, calls this word (coined by Richard Dawkins in his book *The Selfish Gene* in 1976) a "hip word for ideas." Derived from the Greek word meaning memory. A meme is an idea that captures attention and quickly spreads through the Internet (or offline) as the topic du jour.

moblog Combination of "mobile" and "weblog" to mean blogging through mobile devices such as cell phones, BlackBerries, Palm devices and Windows Mobile-based devices.

MSM Acronym for mainstream media, including major newspapers, TV and radio networks.

neighblogs Blogs written by those who are geographically nearby. Not, as you might assume, blogs about horses. Use BlogMap at feedmap.net/BlogMap to find out which of your neighbors are blogging.

old media   See *dead-wood media.*

permalink   Made-up word from the phrase "permanent link." Every blog entry has its own permalink or URL, making that entry its own unique Web page. The proliferation of permalinks (pages) is one of the reasons a blog usually gets high rankings in Google. Also, using a permalink makes it easier to direct someone to a specific blog post even if it's not the most recent one.

ping   A behind-the-scenes network tool that reaches out and touches another network or site by sending a request. Blogs use pings to notify search engines or directories (like Ping-o-matic, blo.gs and Technorati.com) that the blog has been updated. There is no pong. See *trackback.*

P-log   Project blog. Typically an intranet-based blog for project teams to share information related to the blog. Also spelled without the hyphen—Plog.

podcast   An audio file, usually in MP3 format, that can be delivered to your computer through an RSS feed, just like the text entry of a blog. A podcast can be transferred to an iPod or other digital device including other MP3 players, handheld devices and cell phones and listened to at the user's convenience.

post   See *entry.*

reciprocal link   If you post my link, I'll add your link to my blogroll. Scratch my e-back and I'll scratch yours. Also known as link love.

RSS   Technically, a way to transfer information from one computer to another using an XML file. The XML format is very simple. It consists of a headline or title, a summary and a unique link to that specific piece of data or information. RSS stands for Really Simple Syndication. Most commonly, RSS is a "feed" that you subscribe to in order to get updates from a blog or Web site. You can recognize sites and blogs that offer an RSS feed by the little orange RSS or

XML buttons. You can send more than text updates through RSS. Podcasts (MP3) files and vodcasts (video podcasts) can also be transmitted via RSS. The "syndication" piece of the term means that a feed publishes the same update instantly to multiple subscribers or Web pages.

sideblog the content that often appears on the left- or right-hand sides of a blog and contains your blogroll, links to most recent entries and comments, ad sponsorships, calendar, wish lists, and more.

snarky Comments that are considered witty in the blogosphere. Combines sarcastic with cynical. Also, Brit slang.

social media All the tools, including blogs, that enable you to share information, news and opinions online and let others connect with you. Networking on steroids.

splog Stands for spam blog. This has two meanings. One is a blog created for the sole purpose of improving search engine results with fake posts or links. The second one is *comment spam.*

"syndicate this site." Another way of saying that an RSS feed is available for a Web page, Web site or blog. See *RSS.*

tags Keywords or phrases assigned to a blog post, Web site or other online content so that the user, and anyone else, can search on the same tag and find related resources. Del.icio.us, Technorati.com and Flickr.com use tags so visitors can search for identically tagged online articles, audio files, blog entries and photographs.

timestamp Most blog entries include a timestamp indicating the date and sometimes the exact hour of the posting. The timestamp can be manipulated with blogging software, however, so it's possible to pre- and postdate an entry. Not a good alibi.

trackbacks List of other blogs that have linked back to a specific blog entry with commentary. Bloggers often like trackbacks better than comments because they drive traffic back to their blogs.

URL Web address for a site in www.companyname.com format. The address can take you to the Web site or a specific page or file on the site. Not all Web site addresses end with .com. One notorious example: people who want to visit the White House Web site often mistakenly enter .com instead of .gov only to get an unexpected and embarrassing surprise. At least that's what they tell the boss.

vlog   Blog whose entries are video segments. Also known as V-log.

vodcasting   Video on demand broadcasting is much like podcasting except you get video rather than just audio. It's similar to v-log except that the videos aren't necessarily sorted by date like a blog. Personally, I think insiders created the term to confuse those not in the know.

web feed   The generally accepted, non-techie way of saying *RSS*.

web 2.0   Made-up term for what many are calling the next generation of the Web. Refers to a new, more collaborative, interactive and real-time way to use the World Live Web. Lots of mashups and other cool hacks in Web 2.0.

weblog   See *blog*.

wiki   Sounds Polynesian and some claim it derives from the wiki wiki buses at the Honolulu airport. A wiki is a Web page or site that allows users to collaboratively create and edit the editorial content of the page. Wikis are ideal for managing and sharing large amounts of information on a specific topic. A group of hard-working individuals created a comprehensive Hurricane Katrina wiki several days after the single greatest natural disaster to strike the United States.

wikipedia.com   the volunteer-edited online encyclopedia. In 2005 Wikipedia.com became one of the top ten online destinations for news and information. A great place to look up new techie terms or anything I forgot to include in this glossary.

word of mouth (WOM)   When someone spreads information about a product or service to a friend or colleague through on- or off-line communication. Face-to-face, by the water cooler, through blogging, email, text messages, and more.

word of mouth marketing (WOMM)   Can happen two ways. Naturally, through viral marketing. Or by offering incentives to pass on positive reviews to friends and colleagues about an event, product or service. See womma.org.

XML   Stands for eXtreme Markup Language. You often see orange XML buttons on a blog or Web site. They're the same as orange RSS icons, just labeled differently. To be precise, RSS is a subset of XML. Behind the button is the special code to add to your RSS newsreader so you can subscribe to news and updates from this particular feed. See also *RSS* and *Syndicate this site.*

Acknowledgments

What a remarkable coincidence that my childhood friend Elizabeth Wales happens to be a talented literary agent. She prodded me to turn my dream of writing a book into reality and, of course, helped make it happen. (I know Tom Wales will derive particular pleasure from our collaboration.) Equal thanks go to Megan Casey (formerly a senior editor with Penguin Portfolio, now with Squidoo.com), who believed in me and encouraged me with her keen insights and deft editing. I can't say enough good things about the wonderful team at Portfolio—Adrian Zackheim, Adrienne Schultz, Will Weisser and Liz Hazelton. Thanks also to Meryl K. Evans, researcher extraordinaire, for her willingness to take on any request.

In addition, I want to thank loads of other colleagues and friends who helped via their support and encouragement. The list is too long to name everyone (and I'm bound to forget someone). A few people I especially want to mention: Seth Godin, who published an embryonic version of this book on ChangeThis.com and who continues to inspire me with his provocative thinking and generous spirit.

My fellow contributors to BusinessBlogConsulting.com, including Toby Bloomberg, Rich Brooks, Rick Bruner, D. L. Byron, Paul Chancy, Josh Hallett, John Jantsch, Tris Hussey, Dave Taylor, Jim Turner, Dana VanDen Heuvel, Des Walsh, and Jeremy Wright. For inspiration and/or generosity: Mark Amtower, Rebecca Blood, Bob Bly, Aimee Kessler-Evans, John Robertson, Stephan Spencer and Ralph F. Wilson.

The dozens of interviewees who submitted patiently to my questions: especially Matt Blumberg, Philippe Boremanns, Tim Collins, Henry Copeland, Anil Dash, Sally Falkow, Bill French, David Gales, Chris Halvorson, Kevin Holland, Denise Howell, Rok Hrastnik, Michael Hyatt, Shel Israel, Mara Levin, Bob Lutz, Hugh Macleod, Jeremiah Owyang, Bob Parsons, John Patrick, Paul Rosenfeld, Steve Rubel, Zane Safrit, Jonathan Schwartz, Robert Scoble, Doc Searls, Dave Sifry, Steve Spangler, Halley Suitt, Donna Tocci, Mena Trott, David Weinberger and Michael Wiley.

The more than 17,500 subscribers worldwide to my e-newsletter, *WordBiz Report,* deserve mention. Without their unflagging loyalty— and high expectations—I would never have written the hundreds of articles about the power of marketing with content (email, a Web site, a blog) that prefigure this book. For a clean well-lit space to work in, the library in St. Michaels, Maryland, and for espresso, the Blue Crab Coffee House next door. Also, of course, "my" Starbucks a block from my home office.

Last but not least, thanks to my large and wonderful extended family including my sister, Amanda; my brothers, Sandy and William; my cousin Robb and especially my parents, Denie and Frank Weil. Finally, thank you to my three amazing children, Eliza, Timothy and Amanda, who inspire me always. And to my husband, Sam, whose support never wavers.

Notes

CHAPTER 1: TOP TWENTY QUESTIONS ABOUT CORPORATE BLOGGING

1. "Measuring the Blogosphere," *New York Times* editorial, August 5, 2005.

2. In his October 2005 "State of the Blogosphere" report, Technorati CEO Dave Sifry counted just under 20 million blogs and said the total number was doubling every five and a half months.

3. In "The State of Blogging" published in January 2005, the Pew Internet & American Life Project reported that eight million Americans—7 percent of the 120 million who use the Internet—had created blogs. Download report at pewinternet.org/PPF/r/144/report_display.asp.

4. From the white paper "Trust 'MEdia': How Real People Are Finally Being Heard," by Edelman and Intelliseek, Spring 2005. Download at intelliseek.com/whitepapers.asp#trustmedia.

5. "A Day of Terror: The Talk Online; Web Offers Both News and Comfort," *New York Times*, Sept. 12, 2001.

6. From Dave Winer's blog, "Scripting News," at scripting.com/2001/09/11.html.

7. Thanks to attorney Timothy Jucovy in the Washington, D.C., offices of Covington & Burling for clarifying the notion of putting the legal risks of blogging into two buckets. Phone interview, Sept. 28, 2005.

8. 2005 survey "New Frontiers in Employee Communications" by Edelman at edelman.com/speak_up/empeng/Edelman_Employee_Communications_Trends_Survey_Report_2005.pdf.

9. "Blogging Becomes a Corporate Job," *Wall Street Journal*, May 25, 2005, online at careerjournal.com/salaryhiring/industries/sales/20050531-needleman.html.

10. Find mega listings of Macromedia bloggers at weblogs.macromedia.com/mxna/FeedList.cfm, Microsoft bloggers at blogs.msdn.com/default.aspx and Sun Microsystem bloggers at blogs.sun.com/roller/main.do.

11. A good place to find an updated list of corporate blogs is on the NewPR/Wiki at thenewpr.com.

CHAPTER 2: A QUICK ROMP THROUGH THE CORPORATE BLOGOSPHERE

1. Wil Wheaton, a former child actor known for his role on *Star Trek*, is one of the pioneer bloggers. Inspired by the popularity of his blog, he's written several books including *Just a Geek* (O'Reilly Media, 2004) and *Dancing Barefoot* (O'Reilly Media, 2004). Visit his blog at wilwheaton.net.

2. Rebecca Blood, *The Weblog Handbook* (Perseus Publishing 2002), page 3.

3. Joichi Ito is general manager of international operations for blog search company Technorati and chairman of blogging software company Six Apart Japan. He's a board member of the Internet Corporation For Assigned Names and Numbers (ICANN), responsible for the infrastructure of the Internet. In 2000 he was ranked among the "50 Stars of Asia" by *BusinessWeek*. The World Economic Forum chose him as one of the 100 "Global Leaders of Tomorrow" for 2002.

4. "A Blogger in Their Midst," by Halley Suitt, *Harvard Business Review* (Sept. 2003 issue). This case study is remarkably prescient. It describes an employee, "Glove Girl," who undermines the traditional marketing and PR of the fictional medical device company she works for by publishing her own popular blog without the knowledge of her boss.

5. You can download the June 2005 Economist Intelligence Unit study, "Managing Knowledge for Competitive Advantage," at graphics.eiu.com/files/ad_pdfs/Tata_KnowHow_WP.pdf. Courtesy of Sally Falkow and her article, "Sharing Knowledge With A Corporate Blog" in WebProNews.com, Oct. 20, 2005.

6. "To Blog or not to Blog" by P. G. Daly, IntranetJournal.com, Jan. 10, 2005.

7. Information about Google Love Notes courtesy of Susan Solomon, author of the article "Whose Blog Is It Anyway?" published on MarketingProfs.com, April 19, 2005.

8. Stanford University case study courtesy of SixApart.com. MIT Sloan School of Management case study from *Business Blogs: A Practical Guide* by Bill Ives, PhD and Amanda Watlington, PhD (e-book available at BusinessBlogGuide.com, pages 8–9).

9. Case study on German investment bank from Fredrik Wackå at corporate blogging.info/2005/02/internal-blogs-and-wikis-at-bbc.asp.

10. Case study on Ziff Davis Media at socialtext.com/customers/customerziff.

11. Sidebar by corporate communications consultant Shel Holtz. Visit his site at holtz.com.

12. Phone interview with IBM's Philippe Borremans, Oct. 4, 2005.

13. Email interview with Chrysler's Ed Garsten, Sept. 25, 2005.

CHAPTER 3: CONFRONTING FEAR OF BLOGGING

1. "Attack of the Blogs," *Forbes* magazine cover story, Nov. 14, 2005

2. Ibid.

3. Email interview with Forrester's Charlene Li, Oct. 3, 2005.

4. Phone interview with GM's Gary Grates, June 8, 2005.

5. Robert Scoble, Oct. 19, 2004 on his Scobleizer blog at radio.weblogs.com/0001011/2004/10/19.html#a8431.

6. 65% of the 708 readers of WordBiz Report who responded to a "One-Minute Blogging Survey" in July and August 2005 said fear of the time involved was their number one concern about blogging. WordBiz Report subscribers are a mix of Fortune 1000 and small business marketers. Details at blogwriteforceos.com/blogwrite/2005/08/time_still_the_.html.

7. Results of 2005 Backbone Blogging Survey are online at backbonemedia.com/blogsurvey/15-Risks-of-corporate-blog.htm.

8. *Wired* magazine: "Bloggers Suffer Burnout," July 8, 2004.

9. Ibid.

10. Email interview with Bob Lutz, Oct. 25, 2005.

11. "What Blogs Cost American Business," *AdAge.com*, Oct. 24, 2005.

12. Phone interview with Reed Smith appellate and intellectual property attorney Denise Howells, on Sept. 28, 2005. Visit her Bag and Baggage blog at bgbg.blogspot.com.

13. Edelman 2005 survey "New Frontiers in Employee Communications Survey."

14. Phone interview with Mara B. Levin, partner with Herrick, Feinstein LLP, Sept. 28, 2005.

15. For a list of "blogophobic" companies who have fired, disciplined or "not hired" bloggers, see rights.journalspace.com/?b=1104566400&e=1105171200.

16. You can read Plaxo's communication policy online at blog.plaxoed.com/2005/03/29/plaxoscommunication-policy.

17. Laundry list of legal issues from March 2005 Blogging Alert distributed electronically by Howard Rice Attorneys at howardrice.com/uploads/content/Blogging Alert0305.htm.

18. Phone interview with Kryptonite's Donna Tocci, Nov. 3, 2005.

CHAPTER 4: A BAKER'S DOZEN: 12 PLUS 1 WAYS TO USE A CORPORATE BLOG

1. Bill Gates' quote is from Tony Perkins' column "Tune In—Turn On," *Always On* magazine, Spring 2005. As reported by Shel Israel at redcouch.typepad.com/weblog/2005/04/gates_says_most.html.

2. You can find the complete text of Bob Lutz's first entry on the FastLane blog at fastlane.gmblogs.com/archives/2005/01/saturn_product_1.html.

3. Email interview with GM's Michael Wiley, Dec. 2, 2005.

4. Visit Seth Godin's blog at sethgodin.typepad.com.

5. Find Alan Meckler's blog at weblogs.jupitermedia.com/meckler; Matt Blumberg's blog at onlyonce.blogs.com/onlyonce; Mark Cuban's blog at blogmaverick.com; Bob Parsons's blog at bobparsons.com and Mena Trott's blog at sixapart.com/about/corner.

6. Macromedia case study courtesy of Backbone Media's 2005 Corporate Blogging Survey at backbonemedia.com/blogsurvey/47-macromedia-case-study.htm.

7. Macromedia's blog aggregator page is at weblogs.macromedia.com/mxna/FeedList.cfm.

8. Microsoft case study is from Backbone Media's 2005 Corporate Blogging Survey at backbonemedia.com/blogsurvey/52-Microsoft-case-study.htm.

9. For my complete profile of the launch of the QuickBooks Online blog, see blogwriteforceos.com/blogwrite/2005/04/case_study_all_.html.

10. Thanks to Toby Bloomberg of DivaMarketing.com for her profiles of the March of Dimes and American Cancer Society blogs. More case studies about non-profit blogs at bloombergmarketing.blogs.com.

11. You can visit Amnesty International's blogs at blogs.amnestyusa.org.

12. Phone interview with Cheryl Contee, Dec. 21, 2005.

13. Phone interview with David Krane, Google VP of Corporate Communications, Oct. 7, 2005.

14. Phone interview with Chris Halvorson, Oct. 12, 2005.

15. Phone interview with J. D. Iles, Oct. 10, 2005.

16. Hugh Macleod is a curmudgeon cartoonist, marketing consultant, and blogger based in the U.K. This is an adapted version with Hugh's permission; to read the complete riff, go to gapingvoid.com/Moveable_Type/archives/001976.html.

17. "Behaviors of the Blogosphere: Understanding the Size, Composition and Activities of Weblog Readers," ComScore Networks report, August 2005.

18. "Brand Blogs Capture the Attention of Some Companies," by Tania Ralli, *New York Times*, Oct. 24, 2005.

19. Email interview with B. L. Ochman, Dec. 17, 2005.

20. Phone interview with Return Path CEO Matt Blumberg, Oct. 26, 2005.

CHAPTER 5: SHOULD THE CEO BLOG?

1. "If You Want to Lead, Blog" by Jonathan Schwartz, *Harvard Business Review*, November 2005 issue, page 30.

2. PR Week/Burson-Marsteler 2005 CEO Survey (press release) at ceogo.com/pages/press/pr_110705.

3. Chris Brownrigg spoke at the Blog Business Summit in San Francisco, August 2005.

4. "Beware the CEO blog" by Seth Godin on his blog at sethgodin.typepad.com on Oct. 24, 2004.

5. The Business Roundtable is an association of 160 CEOs of the largest corporations in America.

6. "The Open Inbox," *Wall Street Journal*, Oct. 10, 2005.

7. Excerpts from Intel CEO Paul Otellini's internal blog can be downloaded at blogwriteforceos.com/blogwrite/files/blog0215.pdf.

8. Interview with Mena Trott of SixApart, San Francisco, Aug. 16, 2005.

9. Phone interview with Halley Suitt, Aug. 12, 2005.

10. From the article "If You Want to Lead, Blog" by Jonathan Schwartz, *Harvard Business Review*, November 2005.

11. According to one survey of 750 senior executives in the United States, the

United Kingdom, South Africa and Australia, 83 percent of the respondents said their blogs "were written or drafted by someone else, although they approved the text before it was published." More details at www.writer4business.com/bosses_blogs.htm. As with any blogging survey, take the results with a grain of salt.

12. Phone interview with Intel's Tom Beermann, Sept. 28, 2005.

13. First entry on Randy Baseler's blog on Jan. 17, 2005 at boeing.com/randy.

14. Inaugural entry on Jonathan Schwartz's blog on June 28, 2004 at blogs.sun.com/jonathan.

15. Unpublished interview with JupiterMedia CEO Alan Meckler, *BusinessWeek's* Blogspotting.net blog, April 27, 2005.

16. Transcribed from Bob Lutz's first podcast, September 22, 2005. Download the audio file from his blog at fastlane.gmblogs.com/archives/2005/09/first_podcast_w_2.html.

17. Phone interview with Michael Hyatt, Nov. 3, 2005.

18. Karen Christensen is quoted in the article "Why CEOs Should Blog" by Jeneane D. Sussum. Article is online at globalprblogweek.com/2005/09/19/sessum-why-ceos-should-blog. Karen's blog is at berkshirepublishing.com/blog.

19. Email interview with Mark Cuban, Sept. 8, 2005. Visit his blog at blogmaverick.com.

20. GoDaddy.com, a private company with about $200 million in revenues, is the world's third-largest domain name registrar. Read founder Bob Parson's blog at bobparsons.com.

21. Phone interview with Matt Blumberg, Oct. 26, 2005.

22. Phone interview with Zane Safrit, Sept. 16, 2005. Visit his blog at zane.typepad.com/ccuceo.

CHAPTER 6: THE NEW ROI IS ROB (RETURN ON BLOG)

1. "Home-brew iPod Ad Opens Eyes," *Wired* magazine, Dec. 13, 2004. The video is no longer posted to Masters's blog but you can view it at wired.com/news/mac/0,2125,66001,00.html.

2. Email interview with IBM's Christopher Barger, Dec. 15, 2005.

3. HP's Scott Anderson made these remarks at the Syndicate.com conference in San Francisco in December, 2005. Credit to Jeremiah Owyang for taking notes on the speech: jeremiahthewebprophet.blogspot.com/2005/12/notes-from-syndication-conference.html.

4. HP's Rich Marcello blogs at hp.com/blogs/marcello.

5. Email interview with Robert Scoble, Nov. 19, 2005.

6. Email interview with Kevin Holland, Nov. 20, 2005.

7. Phone interview with J. D. Iles, 2005.

8. Blog schwag details from "The Hidden T-shirt Economy," *Business 2.0* magazine, Oct. 25, 2005

9. Phone interview with Michael Wiley, General Motors' Director of New Media, July 15, 2005.

11. "The Secret Sauce for any Corporate Blog," by Steve Rubel, Oct. 31, 2005 on his blog MicroPersuasion.com.

12. Phone interview with Pete Blackshaw, Dec. 1, 2005.

13. Email interview with Robert Scoble, Nov. 19, 2005.

14. "Trust 'MEdia': How Real People Are Finally Being Heard," white paper published by Intelliseek and Edelman in 2005.

15. AOL Blog Trends Survey, published September 2005.

16. Phone interview with Pat Cleary, Oct. 5, 2005.

CHAPTER 7: TOP TEN TIPS TO WRITE AN EFFECTIVE BUSINESS BLOG

1. Lyrics from "Come From the Heart" by Kathy Mattea (1989). The rest of the song goes: "Sing like you don't need the money . . . Love like you'll never get hurt."

2. Email interview with Gerry McGovern, Dec. 21, 2005.

3. Rebecca Blood is author of *The Weblog Handbook* (Perseus Publishing, 2002).

4. Phone interview with Chris Halvorson, chief blogger for Stonyfield Farm, Oct. 12, 2005.

5. Email interview with Denali Flavors' executive vice president John Nardini, Nov. 26, 2005. Visit his blogs at FreeMoneyFinance.com and TeamMooseTracks.com.

6. From Kevin Holland's Associationinc.com blog, Aug. 11, 2005. Read his complete riff on the "Art of Controversy" at www.associationinc.com/blog/index.php/134.

7. Email interview with Doc Searls, June 30, 2005.

8. Blog entry at joi.ito.com/archives/2005/10/10/blogging-style.html

9. "A Plain English Handbook: How to Create Clear SEC Disclosure Documents" by the U.S. Securities and Exchange Commission, Office of Investor Education and Assistance, August 1998: http://www.sec.gov/pdf/handbook.pdf, p. 8.

10. Phone interview with Noel Hartzell, Oct. 12, 2005.

11. Netscape's "What's New" page is archived at wp.netscape.com/home/whats new. It's a fascinating glimpse of the simpler Web that was.

12. "What the In-Crowd Knows: From Hollywood to Wall Street—Our Guide to the Blogs Insiders Read to Stay Current," *Wall Street Journal*, November 16, 2005; Page D1.

13. Amy Gahran's seven-part series on "Blogging Style: The Basic Posting Formats" can be found at blog.contentious.com/archives/2004/09/22/blogging-style-the-basic-posting-formats-series-index.

14. From David Pollard's How to Save the World blog at blogs.salon.com/0002007.

15. Email interview with Michael Hyatt, Dec. 28, 2005.

CHAPTER 8: WHAT YOU REALLY NEED TO KNOW ABOUT BLOGGING TOOLS AND TECHNOLOGY

1. Phone interview with State Farm's Kelly Thul, Feb. 10, 2006.

2. Examples of RSS readers that you download to your desktop are newsgator.com (integrates with Microsoft Outlook) and NetNewsWire (for Mac) at ranchero.com/

netnewswire. Web-based RSS readers include bloglines.com, myyahoo.com, pluck. com and rojo.com.

3. October 2005 RSS study by Yahoo and Ipsos Insight: publisher.yahoo.com/ rss/RSS_whitePaper1004.pdf

4. "RSS and Email: How They Can Work Together," by Rok Hrastnik, Aug. 29, 2005 at rssdiary.marketingstudies.net.

5. Seth Godin's explanation of RSS posted to his blog on August 30, 2005 at sethgodin.typepad.com.

6. Read my two-part profile of Steve Rubel and his "blogging playbook" at blogwriteforceos.com/blogwrite/2005/08/steve_rubel_rev.html.

7. "Email Is So Five Minutes Ago," *BusinessWeek*, Nov. 28, 2005.

8. The Fortune 500 Blogging Index has another motive as well—to test the hypothesis that large companies whose financial performance is on a downward slope are more likely to blog. Only 24 out of the Fortune 500s were recorded as having public blogs in March 2006. So not enough data to draw any final conclusions. Visit the index at socialtext.net/bizblogs/index.cgi.

9. Wikipedia ranked number eight in Nielsen/NetRatings' Top 10 Online News & Information Destinations, Nov. 22, 2005: www.imediaconnection.com/content/ 7322.asp

10. Peruse Steve Rubel's lists of Ten Hacks at blogwriteforceos.com/blogwrite/ 2005/11/steve_rubels_te.html.

CHAPTER 9: CHEAT SHEET: HOW TO MAKE THE CASE FOR BLOGGING TO THE BOSS

1. "If a magazine is cutting staffers, can it afford to increase blogging?" by Stephen Baker, Blogspotting.net, Dec. 31, 2005.

2. BLOG = Better Listings on Google, courtesy of Rick Bruner, Executive Summary.com and director of research, DoubleClick.net.

3. "Attack of the Blogs," *Forbes* magazine cover story, Nov. 14, 2005.

4. Waggoner Edstrom's Blogging Index is at waggeneredstrom.com/what_we_ do/expertise/blogging/blog_index.htm. You can fill it out online to tote up your "blogging readiness" score.

5. Email interview with Laurie Mayers, Dec. 18, 2005.

6. Blog entry by Richard Edelman on how to select a corporate blogger, Dec. 19, 2005 at www.edelman.com/speak_up.

7. Executive Summary PowerPoint slide, dated Dec. 15, 2004, provided by Michael Wiley, General Motors' Director of New Media.

CHAPTER 10: WHAT'S NEXT

1. David St Lawrence, from his Ripples: post-corporate adventures blog at ripples.typepad.com/ripples.

2. You'll find a good explanation of the Long Tail, with an illustration of the demand curve, at squidoo.com/longtail. The Long Tail is a term coined by *Wired*

founding editor Chris Anderson in 2004. Also see his book, *The Long Tail* by Chris Anderson (Hyperion, 2006).

3. "Welcoming citizen marketers into your world," by Jackie Huba on her blog at customerevangelists.typepad.com, Feb. 14, 2005. Jackie is coauthor with Ben McConnell of *Creating Customer Evangelists* (Kaplan Publishing, 2003).

4. Download Edelman's 2006 Trust Barometer from edelman.com.

5. *The World Is Flat*, by Thomas L. Friedman, p.153 (Farrar, Straus and Giroux, 2005).

6. Interview with Technorati's Peter Hirshberg, July 13, 2005.

7. "Teen Content Creators and Consumers," Pew Internet & American Life Project, November 2005. Download at pewinternet.org.

Index